be aware that when bullying become
of a child, who then feels worthless :
chological effects which can create
extend into adulthood.

D1459061

Dr Sam has highlighted the telltale signs for adults to notice when their child is going through a turbulent time, such as depression, self-harm, absences from school, change of behaviour and so on. 'Bullying is behaviour by an individual or group, repeated over time, that intentionally hurts another individual or group either physically or emotionally.' It couldn't have been put in simpler terms.

Dr Sam provides perfect examples of children who grow to be bullies and mistake it for leadership skills. That is why the role of parents and carers is essential in providing guidance. She touches upon every angle to provide a good read and educate those who are in a position to reduce any sort of bullying. Cyberbullying is the new trend so there is an in-depth chapter on how parents/carers can monitor this.

Jas Bassi BSc, Clinical Hypnotist

Some may question why this singular view on bullying is necessary in an age of 'equality of opportunity' and 'equal rights'. This book goes straight to the heart of the matter: girls practise and rehearse social relationships with an intensity unmatched by your average boy. Personal and intimate information exchanged 'in confidence' and 'in friendship' can then become a weapon more brutal than a fist or a hammer.

The author develops compelling imagery of girl-on-girl bullying through the enrolment of others as akin to how a wolf pack operates. This may seem extreme; in my opinion, it needs to be said. Bullying is personally experienced and personally wounding. The psychological damage is profound, life-lasting and life-changing.

The author goes on to explore the impact of bullying when 'manipulation of friendship' seeps into cyberspace. The number of young females taking their lives because of cyberbullying is increasing: we must develop a sharper and more nuanced view of the problem before we work towards effective solutions.

The book does a good job in this respect. A call for the modelling of pro-social behaviours, building a school or college community with built-in reporting structures, proactive peer support, victim support and developing an ethos that breaks the code of silence are all sound anti-bullying strategies.

I also agree wholeheartedly with the moral imperative that runs through this book: some schools are frightened to exert their influence and authority beyond the classroom, the playground or the school gate. It is time for courageous, open leadership to reduce the impact and incidence of bullying on the well-being, life-course and achievement of young people. This book will help.

Marius Frank, Materials Director, Achievement for All

Dr Sam has a wealth of experience in responding to bullying and in providing support, training and development to parents and those working with young people. Her warmth, empathy and knowledge is evident in *Girl Bullying*. This will be reassuring to readers who are seeking to understand and tackle the complex and dark world of bullying children, particularly girls. Readers will be given confidence to tackle this difficult subject.

In *Girl Bullying*, Dr Sam is taking a fresh approach in focusing on girl bullying and analysing the experience of both girls who are victims and those who are perpetrators. Gender is a key factor in social interactions and it is helpful to consider this in the context of bullying. It is also useful to spotlight girls because we know from the children and young people contacting ChildLine that more than twice as many girls are counselled by the helpline as boys about bullying and online bullying. ChildLine has seen a very significant increase in the number of girls talking about feeling excluded or isolated as a result of being bullied. Confirming Dr Sam's approach, ChildLine has also seen a large increase in concerns about cyberbullying. *Girl Bullying* addresses these issues in detail in relation to girls, emphasising that young people do not differentiate between the online and offline worlds.

A strength of *Girl Bullying* is that the author relates the experience of bullying to child and adolescent development. This provides important insights into why bullying can have such a significant and devastating impact on the well-being of those affected. Bullying can affect a child's development, self-esteem, confidence and capacity to form relationships. Sadly, too many professionals and others working with young people lack a good understanding of child development and *Girl Bullying* will help meet a real need.

Using case studies and the results of consultations with children and young people, Dr Sam offers a comprehensive approach to tackling bullying. She rightly argues that bullying needs to be addressed holistically at a number of different levels and there is a vital need to be proactive in preventing bullying happening in the first place. Dr Sam provides detailed strategies based on placing victims' views and experiences at the centre.

Christopher Cloke, Head of Safeguarding in Communities,
NSPCC, Former Chair, Anti-Bullying Alliance

GIRL BULLYING

DR SAM

Crown House Publishing Limited
www.crownhouse.co.uk

First published by

Crown House Publishing Limited
Crown Buildings, Bancyfelin, Carmarthen, Wales, SA33 5ND, UK
www.crownhouse.co.uk

and

Crown House Publishing Company LLC
6 Trowbridge Drive, Suite 5, Bethel, CT 06801, USA
www.crownhousepublishing.com

British Library Cataloguing-in-Publication Data

A catalogue entry for this book is available from the British Library.

Print ISBN 978-184590953-6
Mobi ISBN 978-178583028-0
ePub ISBN 978-178583029-7
ePDF ISBN 978-1785830030-3

LCCN 2015951245

Edited by Nick Owen

Printed and bound in the UK by
Gomer Press, Llandysul, Ceredigion

FOREWORD

Right from the start, this book engages us with a convincing mix of pupil voice, personal experience and thoughtful comments on the important topic of girl bullying. The author brings many years of experience in anti-bullying work, and in educational and therapeutic work with schools and with young people. This pays off in terms of the range of thoughtful advice she gives on dealing with the issues. However, the book is also enlivened and enriched by the material from interviews and focus groups with pupils themselves, making for a vivid narrative.

The book is about girls bullying, primarily. To some extent girls bullying is different from boys bullying, tending to be more focused on shifting relationships, denigration and exclusion, rather than the more obvious physical forms. Social relationships in middle childhood and adolescence are now transformed by the widespread use of the internet and social networking sites. The majority of this is enjoyable and can be educational, but as the book makes clear, it can provide opportunities for relationship-based bullying too. The more recent forms of cyberbullying occur with both boys and girls, but there is some evidence that girls are relatively more involved in this than in what has now been called traditional or face-to-face bullying. Nevertheless, there is overlap. Although focused on girls bullying, much of the material, including suggestions for intervention, will apply to bullying generally, whoever is involved.

Whatever forms bullying takes, it is concerned with power and the abuse of power. Leadership, when exercised well, can be a beneficent use of power. But its systematic misuse or abuse signals bullying.

Experiences of being bullied in childhood can have traumatic effects. This, of course, depends on many factors – the kinds and extent of bullying, how long it goes on for, how the victim tries to cope, and what support they get. Some children and young people can cope effectively in some circumstances. But the imbalance of power in bullying makes this difficult. Large-scale and longitudinal surveys have shown how victim experiences can bring about loss of self-esteem, depression and difficulties of trust in relationships – both in the short term, but also, and especially if nothing is done about it, in the longer term. Cases of suicide due – in large part at least – to bullying or cyberbullying bear tragic witness to what can be the outcome. Such cases are thankfully rare, but must be the tip of an iceberg of suffering that many victims experience.

A strength of this book is that nearly half of it is devoted to ways in which young people, parents and schools can work together to reduce bullying and deal with it effectively whenever it occurs. A variety of sensible suggestions are offered, together with a help-ful range of materials in the appendices. I believe the author is right in emphasising the importance of leadership from the sen-ior management of the school. Combining this with a clear school anti-bullying policy (including cyberbullying), adequate ways of reporting bullying, thorough follow-up of incidents, a good rela-tionships curriculum and harnessing the support of the majority of pupils and parents, can make a great difference in levels of bullying and in pupil happiness. This book will surely be a very useful and supportive resource for this endeavour.

Professor Peter K. Smith, Goldsmiths College,
University of London, author of *Understanding School
Bullying: Its Nature and Prevention Strategies*

CONTENTS

PREFACE

I first began to research into the long-term impact of girl bullying eighteen years ago. Sometime after that, I started to run courses, seminars and workshops with school staff on the key issues involved: the cultural aspects, the communication breakdowns and the consequences of bullying. To support this work I also developed a variety of proactive and reactive strategies for schools to implement to deal with the challenge.

At the same time I have also worked therapeutically with young girls and women who have been psychologically damaged by bullying. And that's not just with victims of bullies, but also with the bullies themselves, who often find that their manipulative and calculating behaviours don't serve them well in building satisfying long-term relationships or in matters of self-concept.

Over the years I have often been asked to write a book on the subject, but never quite got around to it for a whole raft of very good reasons. And then two incidents occurred almost simultaneously. The first followed an intense training day I delivered to delegates from many different schools. Most of them were trying to deal with the *pack mentality* of girl bullying: they were all struggling to tackle the issue of girl bullying and how they could deal with it effectively. After the session, they overwhelmed me with requests to write a book on the topic. The second incident was a series of newspaper reports headlining the increasing number of girls committing suicide as a result of being cyberbullied.

I had long been deeply concerned about girl bullying and the damage it causes. These two incidents were the triggers that made up my mind. No more procrastinating. The book was an idea whose time had come. I determined to find the time to complete it and show just how bothered *I* was by the issue, and that I was prepared to do something tangible about it.

Having made up my mind, I wanted to be sure that this book would have real meaning to young people affected by bullying and all its ramifications. I wanted to speak to, and hear the real voices of, bullies, bystanders, and victims alike. I knew it was essential to include the contemporary voices of real young people and adults; those who live with, and deal with, girl bullying, day in and day out.

My research work has always focused on ensuring that the authentic voices of young people are properly represented when it comes to welfare and safeguarding issues. Too often these voices are drowned out by adults and experts, no matter how well-meaning they may be. To this end, I designed a research project called 'Do I Look Bothered? Voices'. Seventy-eight children, young people and adults volunteered to share their views, ideas and experiences about bullying in a variety of different formats. The project took place during the winter and early spring of 2014/2015 and consisted of a survey, focus group discussions, interviews and case studies. All British Psychological Society ethical guidelines were adhered to and consent given for anonymous quotes used here with pseudonyms. Fifty-eight children and young people aged between eight and fifteen took part in the survey. Sixteen thirteen- to fifteen-year-olds participated in various focus group discussions, while others contributed through in-depth case studies and interviews. The latter included two young people aged fifteen and eighteen, a parent and a school staff member. All the young people engaged in the project attended schools in England. Where anonymity has been guaranteed or requested, names and identifying features have been changed.

THANKS AND ACKNOWLEDGEMENTS

I would like to thank every child, young person and adult who, over the years and throughout the writing of this book, has freely given their time and opinions in order to help me remain focused on their perspective, their needs, and their understanding of the issues involved in girl bullying.

Also, I would like to thank my editor, Nick Owen, for his endless patience and thought-provoking comments; Zak Zarychta, for his amazing brain and quantitative analytical skills; and, last but by no means least, my daughters, for accepting that I have had to hide away with my computer for months on end to write this book. I know that I became a virtual mother during this process. Now I can finally re-emerge into the daylight and be a real-life mum again, and a loving Meme to my beautiful granddaughter.

INTRODUCTION

'Sticks and stones may break my bones,
but words will never hurt me.'

Folk wisdom usually has something insightful to say. But not in this case. This sticks and stones stuff is about as devoid of sense and psychological awareness as it's possible to get. There's a crisis going on in our schools and in cyberspace that needs our attention – *now*. Informed action is needed to prevent another generation of young people from becoming distrustful, defensive and psychologically damaged. This situation affects girls and young women in particular.

Here are some statistics. Ditch the Label's Annual Bullying Survey (2014) reported the following:

- 45% of young people have experienced bullying by the age of 18.

- 26% of children report being bullied every day.

- 56% said bullying affected their studies.

- 30% said bullying had led to self-harm.

- 36% said they were bullied about their weight or shape.

- 40% said they were bullied about their appearance.

- 82% had been indirectly bullied (for example, through deliberate social exclusion).

- 30% had had suicidal thoughts.

- 10% had attempted to commit suicide.

An earlier study, BeatBullying (2009), further reported: '44% of child suicides are said to be due to bullying, and 65% of those suicides are committed by girls.'

Bullying, and girl bullying in particular, has to be addressed. We have to begin to understand and learn its real nature.

It's just an ordinary school day like any other. Imagine you're there, one of the students. You're standing in the playground, looking around to see where you can fit in. Have you ever felt that fear? The fear that you just might *not* fit in? It's not so bad in primary school playgrounds, because in primary schools parents and teachers try to determine and engineer friendships. But in secondary school that doesn't work. It doesn't work because it isn't adults who manage the social hierarchy among pupils – it's wolves.

The alpha female dominates the pack. She alone decides who'll be accepted and who she'll reject, who's in and who's out. Perhaps she'll choose you as her beta wolf, her second in command. Perhaps you'll think that's a very safe position to hold. But you'd be wrong. Dead wrong. Nowhere's a safe place to be in the wolf pack's hierarchy. Even the alpha's terrified of demotion. No one's secure. The beta's particularly vulnerable: always at risk of being in the wrong place at the wrong time, of being accused of stabbing the alpha in the back rather than supporting her. Disloyalty, even if only perceived, is one of the worst 'crimes'. The 'beta wolf' is in a precarious position. She'll be used and abused. Her fear of rejection will drive her to do anything to secure her precious safety a little while longer. And make no mistake – the beta wolf's capable of doing anything at all, no matter who gets hurt.

But maybe you'll get passed over for the beta role. Don't worry too much: the alpha female, if she's feeling inclusive, might make you a pack member ... but only so long as you're useful. She might trick you into believing you have some important rank in the hierarchy; a titled position, something worth having. And you'll believe it. Even if that title is 'omega', the lowest ranking wolf in the pack, you'll buy into it for all you're worth because there's no alternative. Let's face it, there's only one rule that matters in the jungle of the playground: *it's better to be in than out*.

Out means out – 'out there', isolated, all alone, abandoned. No one wants to be a lone wolf. Lone wolves are left alone by everyone ... everyone except *her*. The alpha female needs the lone wolf's isolation to remind others what could happen to them. She needs the lone wolf's fear to be sensed, be seen, be felt. Viscerally. The victim shrinks away from the alpha female's glare, her defeated body language unmistakably marking her status as outcast. For the pack, these signals powerfully reinforce who's in charge. And so the alpha female reigns supreme.

Sometimes, to reinforce her power, the alpha likes to toy with her victim. She'll circle her prey, and look her up and down a couple of times. She'll lick her lips, toss her head and then move in, all sweetness and light, making her intended target feel so special as she receives the full force of the alpha's attention. Caught off guard, the victim lets her guard down, trading her fear for her need for friendship. And the alpha will take that trade all day long. She'll let the lone wolf bathe in the glow of her attention; let her bask for a while in the false sense of security that she takes from her proximity to power.

To the alpha, the victim is useful for just as long as she chooses, for as long as it serves her purpose. She'll wait. She'll watch. And when the time is right, and she's ready to feed off the power she craves, the alpha will cut her down. She'll crush her and then walk back to her pack, grinning. She won't need to look back. She'll know how utterly destroyed her victim is. No one will help her, afraid that if they do it will be their turn next. The victim is labelled, marked and, their confidence shattered, cast adrift to their lonely and fearful fate.

No one wants to be a lone wolf, and so the alpha female has many supporters. Some are silent, some skulking in the shadows, some prominent and visible right next to her. They're all hanging in there. Waiting for the order to take the next victim down, to reassert the alpha wolf as queen of the social hierarchy once again. She'll carry on ruling this way just as long as those around her accept the pack and its values – or remain too afraid to challenge her or the system.

Until that happens, more victims will pay the price that she demands. More tragedies will happen; some that will even end in death. They'll happen because our excuses and denials allow them to. They'll happen because too many people who could, and should, take action hide in the shadows, refusing to intervene or take responsibility.

Lack of action creates the vacuum the she-wolf needs to feed on her prey, tells the world that this culture is tolerated and fails to acknowledge the fear that holds the pack in her thrall. 'If only', pack and prey might say, 'she'd been turned around, if only her power had been challenged, if only she'd been stopped.'

We all know that turning a blind eye allows the pack mentality to continue. Yet even with our 'good' eye there are too many times when we just look on as the lives of those outside the pack, and even those within it, are put at risk and damaged, or even destroyed. And the great irony is that this scenario also includes the seemingly untouchable one, the alpha female herself.

If we don't act soon, the consequences will be stark and the price to be paid will be high: young women lacking a healthy self-concept, unable to develop healthy social interactions, never learning that it is mutuality and trust, rather than power, that forms the basis of healthy, long-lasting relationships.

When children and adults begin to think that nothing can be done about the abuse of power, the ritual humiliations, the in-group domination, the abusive friendships and the social 'punishments', including isolation and physical harm, it's clearly time to challenge the trend and take decisive action. It's the very prevalence of inaction that maintains the culture of girl bullying. And this creeping normalisation is why it's so important to tackle it.

PART ONE
GIRL BULLYING

Chapter 1
GIRL BULLYING: WHY ACTION MATTERS

Childhood is central to our personal and social development. The way adults in particular respond to children who are in need of support plays a vital role in helping them understand social and cultural norms: what is right and wrong, what is acceptable and unacceptable behaviour. Every time girl bullying goes unchallenged, and is allowed to continue, it sends out the message that it's OK.

When this becomes the new 'normal' we have a serious cultural problem on our hands, and one that won't be confined only to school playgrounds. We need to understand that this is not only a problem for girls and young women. As they take their place in society it will affect all of us: their families, the culture, and society as a whole.

On a case-by-case basis, it can all seem so ordinary, so everyday, so below the radar. And after all, we're all busy dealing with problems of our own. It's so easy to miss how small, yet deftly timed, acts of power play can cause such confidence-wrecking damage to the integrity and self-belief of an individual. Here's part of Jodie's story. Jodie was one of the lucky ones – she was able to get support and move beyond the paralysis of social isolation.

JODIE'S STORY

When I look back, I was a manipulated fool. I enjoyed being friends with the bully because she was pretty and popular – or so I thought. Throughout our friendship I never knew when I went into school in a morning if she'd be speaking [to me]. It was something I expected. She constantly kept me down, telling me she had been invited to parties and made a big thing that I wasn't invited. I now know the parties didn't exist.

I was at a low time in my life when I needed her support and she chose to ignore me … I wanted her to stop her treating me like this … She told everyone that I'd told her not to speak to me. She followed me at break times saying nasty comments, turned my friends against me, bringing me to an all-time low. I felt the teacher blamed me for everything. I dreaded going to school and my life was a misery. She told people not to invite me to parties and excluded me constantly. I was isolated … I felt worthless.

Jodie was bullied to the point where she lost all her confidence. She hated school, began to work on a reduced timetable and study at home. She never knew when those friends she thought she had would turn on her. She was in high school. She was just at that stage in her life when she should have been learning about who she was and where she fitted in to her social world. Instead, that social world became her worst nightmare. Trying to work out who she was just left her confused and angry.

Every day, girl bullying destroys healthy friendships, self-confidence, self-belief and self-concept. For Jodie, it also affected her trust in those she believed should have been most there to support her at school: the teachers in her life. When she tried to speak to her teachers she got the distinct impression that she was being blamed for not being able to solve the problem herself. Worse still, they led her to believe that *she* was the cause of the problem.

Such confusion and lack of support can make a young person feel invisible, unimportant and incredibly powerless. Like every other child, Jodie should have had the right to feel safe at school and to have had any welfare issues heard with respect and without judgement.

If this lack of due diligence occurred in an adult workplace it would shake our belief in the culture and leadership of that organisation. It would raise serious questions and challenges that could well end up in a court of law. A healthy society is based on safety and trust. Workplace law exists to protect adults from abuse and bullying, and the detrimental effects these behaviours have on our psychological health. If this is true for adults, how much more should it apply to vulnerable young people who are just beginning to develop a sense of identity distinct from that of their family? The high school years are the very ones where young people need most support in learning that trust, mutuality, integrity and respect for self and others (based on shared ethical principles) form the core of healthy, long-lasting relationships and form the basis of a healthy, civilised society.

Sadly, Jodie's experience is not at all unusual. Those of us who have been victims will have been played for a fool, like Jodie, in a social power game. Let's name bullying for what it is: a particularly unpleasant form of social and emotional abuse. At school, many of us were pawns in these games, competing for power and social status. Some of us were victims, while some of us may have been the alpha female or a member of the pack. Whichever role or roles we played – and some of us may well have played both – there can be no doubt that we were diminished or damaged in some way by the roles we took or were given. For the victims like Jodie – manipulated, belittled, isolated, made to feel worthless, held accountable by those she looked to for help, dreading the start of each new day – is it surprising that so many turn to self-harm, or even suicide, to simply have their pain heard and be acknowledged?

Jodie was one of the luckier ones. She found the courage to speak to her family. But even with their support, life at school continued to be difficult. Her faith and trust had been betrayed. Her faith and trust in the loyalty of friends, and her faith and trust in the authorities to act against abusive behaviour and vindictiveness, had been significantly damaged. Above all, she was left with an impression that nothing changes; that the silence and inaction of teachers and other adults are tacit invitations for the wolves to continue their predatory 'games.'

> I have learned a lot of lessons in the last few months. It's been hard but I am stronger. As for [her], she will always be a bully, as no one has ever told her that she is a bully.
>
> **Jodie**

THE WIDER PICTURE

While Jodie's family were more than willing to listen to her and give her the support she needed, many young people are not so lucky. For whatever reasons, some families just don't seem to want to get involved or take the issues seriously. They may not know how to respond, they may not feel it's important enough to react or they may simply not see anything wrong in bullying behaviour, especially if there's a history of it in the family. This refusal to get involved or take matters seriously only compounds the problem. When a young person in need feels that those they trust most are unwilling to hear them or value their perspective, it can have devastating consequences. It sends out a message to the child that they are not worthy of support. When they get the same message from friends and teachers, it's not surprising that they may feel totally isolated, worthless and cast adrift. They can simply feel they have no one to turn to.

So who is responsible for all the damage that is being caused, often in plain sight? The young people or the adults? Or do we all bear some responsibility? This is not a time for blame but for action that addresses the causes of the problem, not just the symptoms. And we need to embrace the whole picture; to recognise that it's not just the socially isolated child, but also the socially powerful bully, who are in desperate need of help to learn different lessons. They should both be offered the chance to learn how to develop healthy, respectful, mutual relationships in which disagreement and conflict can be addressed through dialogue and other acceptable channels. In fact, many of us need to develop our skills in this area. It's one of the great challenges we face in the twenty-first century. Taking action on girl bullying is as good a place as any to start a shift in our thinking and actions.

That shift is something fairly new, but the problem is as old as the hills. Power has always played a central role in the playground, in social groups and in clubs. It was certainly the case when I was young and, I imagine, when my mother and grandmother were teenagers. But when I was young the power games only really affected me and my generation in public spaces: at school, at the youth club, at Brownies or Guides or when we were playing in the streets or the play park.

And although there was no internet in those days, and therefore no cyberbullying relentlessly operating 24/7, the power games and the bullying were still present. I can still remember my fear of the alpha female's glare, her ability to take my friends away and leave me alone and isolated. I remember other times, when I was invited into her pack, laughing with her at the victims we picked on, and then expelled from the pack, laughed at and mocked by her and her cronies.

To my shame, I also remember very clearly trying to get a taste of that power for myself. It was only a fleeting taste, though, because I had no pack to follow me. But how I longed to sense some of that self-validating power for myself. If only I could get my own back by finding someone smaller than myself. And I did. She was certainly smaller than me ... but unfortunately for me (or perhaps fortunately), her older brother wasn't! He sent me a threat which almost stopped me ever going to school again, and which certainly stopped me ever again considering getting involved in bullying behaviour. I was too scared to look at anyone after that, nicely or nastily.

I learned some really powerful lessons from these experiences. I realised that I had no real power to begin with, and at the end I had even less, because to be a bully I needed supporters. I needed an audience. I needed to be someone ... and at that time I wasn't.

So how does the alpha female gain her status? How does she gain pre-eminence in her territory and over her pack? It strikes me that it's a bit like being a celebrity. Write a few tweets, say a few things to impress, do a few bad things and make them high profile, and you have yourself a *persona*. There's always going to be people who are impressed with stuff like that: hangers-on, those who want to know you, be seen with you, be associated with you. And if your persona is popular and you can prove your social power, you gather the pack around you and your status is set. The pack lurks in your shadow, unconsciously reinforcing your social status.

This is a moment when a teacher might spot the bullying and talk to the bully and the victim. But talking rarely works. 'Let's shake hands and move on' rarely works – because it neither addresses the imbalance of power or the relative status that exists between the bully and the bullied. Bullying is far more complex than a simple dispute between a perpetrator and a victim. That's why so often nothing changes and the behaviour continues. Bullying demands us to examine the nature and dynamics of power as it exists in the playground, in our families, in social forums, in the media and in our culture.

THE DYNAMICS OF POWER

As young people begin to dis-identify from their parents and siblings, they look to establish their own sense of self. Who am I and how am I different from others? There is a natural sense of individual power that arises in this. It is normal and at its best it is healthy.

However, this use of power can easily become opportunistic. Unless the child has good role models – from home, school and even from the media – about how to build effective and mutual social relationships, this new sense of power can easily become unhealthy and abusive in social contexts and relationships.

The problem is that effective, healthy role models are all too often lacking. At the same time, the child needs ongoing coaching and modelling about what is and is not acceptable social behaviour, so that power is related to personal responsibility. And at the same time the child needs support to develop the ability to notice, challenge and critique the unhealthy models so often prevalent in playground, the media and the wider world.

We are not tackling girl bullying effectively. We are not linking the behaviours to the natural confusion some young people have about how to work with their newly emerging sense of personal power and how much help and support they need with this. Nor are we linking the behaviours to the broader social issues: the existence of negative role models in many homes, the media and even in schools; the unwillingness of many people in authority to acknowledge that a serious problem exists; the lack of deep and sensitive listening when vulnerable children find the courage to express themselves; and the consequent widespread fear of not being heard, or being seen as a 'snitch', that stops children reporting cases of bullying. These are some, but by no means all, of the reasons why it is the unhealthy version of social power that continues to dominate in so many playgrounds.

We can begin to redress the balance by working with these two areas. First, we should recognise that children need exposure to excellent models of social interaction, to which the whole school is aligned, and an awareness that straying from these models is unacceptable and will not be tolerated. Second, we need to own the fact that much of the destructive behaviour that goes on in schools and beyond is reinforced by what children observe in the adult world: we need to look at our own behaviours, including silence and inaction, and we need to look at the role of the media.

We can't deal with these complex issues simply by talking at or to the victims and perpetrators as if they are isolated incidents. We need to have a much more structured and aligned response. 'Shooting from the hip' and knee-jerk reactions don't solve anything. Often they compound the problem because they fail to address the underlying issues. They change nothing in the long run. And every time they fail, the power of the alpha female increases its strength and its hold over the victims.

So what can we do?

We need to start being *proactive* rather than *reactive*. We need to start thinking big – way beyond the confines of the box that we've got ourselves into through confusion and inaction. We need to ask ourselves how it is that social power is abused so freely and that it so often goes unchallenged. We need to stop accepting things as they are. We need to stop condoning bullying as something that is just a normal part of adolescence. We need to recognise the crippling effects girl bullying has on *everyone* caught up in it, including the alpha females. We need to name bullying for what it is: unacceptable emotional and social abuse, harassment, character defamation, slander. Above all, we need to stop negating our responsibility by making the callow excuse that it is just 'girls being girls'. Now is the time to stop applying short-term solutions that will not only fail but will likely make the problem worse.

THE FALLOUT

I've worked with many women who have suffered problems in their adult life, problems that can frequently be traced back to bullying at home or at school. It's not at all unusual for girls who were bullied by their female peers to carry the psychological scars into their adult lives. Their low levels of self-confidence and self-esteem, in particular, contribute directly to conditions that create unhealthy adult relationships. They recall very clearly the lack of support they felt; their sense of worthlessness that their hurt and humiliation were not taken seriously. Often they came to feel that they were insignificant and that their pain wasn't 'real'. These early brutal 'lessons' from the playground can leave hugely damaging scars. They can create a wholly negative map of what they think they should and should not accept, and what they should and should not tolerate in a relationship. As a consequence, these women lack high expectations about how they deserve to be treated. Dignity, respect and mutuality are words that may not feature in their understanding of what it means to have a healthy relationship.

Some of the most damaged women I've worked with were girl bullies themselves. They also failed to develop a healthy view of friendship, loyalty and trust. I once heard the story of a girl who had bullied at school. Years later she came face to face with one of her victims, and made a telling and painful confession. She told

her former 'victim' that she felt she was being 'paid back' for her bad behaviour. At the school they attended, her two daughters were suffering at the hands of a bully. It seems that very few girls involved in bullying get to walk away undamaged.

Suicide, long-term psychological damage, guilt, hurt, fear, lack of trust and openness, regret, limiting and limited personal relationships are all elements of the fallout of bullying in all its many forms. The collateral damage caused, not by sticks and stones, but by the 'names' and 'looks' that are meant to never hurt us, is massive – and the legacy can last a lifetime.

Perhaps things are beginning to change. The relatively new phenomenon of cyberbullying is a perfect arena for girls to bully other girls. But it is something we can begin to act on, and it also suggests why we have found it so hard to crack down on traditional bullying in the past. Cyberbullying is both visible and traceable. It offers hard evidence about what is being done to whom and by whom. Bullying in the playground, on the other hand, is much subtler. It's conducted through looks, body language and subtle put-downs. It's not always easily visible and rarely generates witnesses who are prepared to talk about it. It's often diffused through the behaviours of the whole pack rather than just the alpha female. And there are (usually) no physical bruises.

But as we all know, the difficulty of collecting evidence doesn't mean that nothing is happening. The scale of cyberbullying indicates just how big a problem we have on our hands. We need to be more vigilant in noticing the subtle signals and the evidence generated by behavioural changes in those who are being bullied: falling grades, increasing absences from school, illnesses, depression, self-harm.

We compound the problem every time we fail to notice these things or fail to enquire about the causes. We compound it every time we walk past the child who avoids lunchtimes and would rather pick up litter in the school corridors, either not 'seeing' them or persuading ourselves that this is normal behaviour.

Let's face it, girl bullying happens because we allow it to. It happens because too many people who should know better prefer to take the easy option and look the other way or fool themselves that it's not so serious. It happens because too many people have preferred the easy-to-enforce liberal frame of 'personal choice' over the basic human right of children to develop in safety and security. The anarchy of the playground run by the wolf pack has to be challenged. The road ahead requires tough love and tough choices: above all, it requires the recognition that there are certain social norms and rules that are essential for the healthy social development of young people; that rules and social conventions about what is acceptable and what is not, about equality, respect and mutuality, are the glue that holds civilised society together.

This won't happen by itself. It will require effort and energy. It will require skills in giving unequivocal and compassionate feedback about behaviours. But it has to be done. Anything less would be a dereliction of duty towards future generations.

The question is: how many broken lives and suicides will it take before we finally wake up to the challenge we all face?

Chapter 2

SO WHAT IS BULLYING?
A DEFINITION PROBLEM

INTRODUCTION

In this chapter I'll explore the current confusion around definitions of bullying and some of the reasons why such a lack of clarity exists. I'll look at the different elements that constitute bullying behaviour, especially girl bullying and indirect bullying. At the end I'll attempt to come up with a definition that embraces all these elements and upon which we can begin to build a strategy that will enable us to tackle bullying in a structured and comprehensive way.

There are many different views, perspectives and definitions about what bullying is and isn't. When it comes to girl bullying, those differences not only multiply but morph into utter confusion. In the past it's been hard enough to reach any agreement on what constitutes physical bullying, so when it comes to indirect bullying, cyberbullying and girl bullying, where the manipulation of power is so much more subtle, reaching agreement becomes very much more difficult.

Not long ago I decided to explore these issues and the confusion that surrounds them with some of my international students. I wanted to find out how perceptions of bullying differ across cultures and how we could help students who were being bullied. We discussed the UK Department for Education (2015) definitions of bullying, and some of my international students were more than a little shocked and surprised.

Many of them said that an adult hitting a child to establish authority was acceptable in their country. They also said the same was true for older brothers and sisters coercing their younger siblings or even younger others. Some of these students could not see why someone more powerful hitting another less powerful in this context was an issue worth raising. Only a few agreed that verbal and psychological intimidation was bullying. I then talked about the UK's safeguarding policies for children and, as you can imagine, there were more raised eyebrows.

I took three things away from that session. First, an awareness of just how markedly views can differ across cultures. Second, that I could at least take some comfort that the UK does have stringent safeguarding policies in place, even if they are not always as clear as many of us would like them to be. Most important of all, though, what I learned was that a very large gap exists between definitions, theory and practice.

If we are going to address girl bullying, we have to understand that it is, first and foremost, a safeguarding issue. Children, and especially vulnerable children, need to be protected. But to achieve this we need clear definitions. The problem is that, while direct, physical bullying is easily seen and evidenced, and relatively easily defined, no such clarity exists when it comes to indirect methods of bullying. And it is these indirect methods – a put-down, a glance, a sarcastic tone, social exclusion from the 'in' crowd – that are among the strategies that girl bullies skilfully and maliciously use to maintain their status at the head of the pack.

Taken alone, each item can seem insignificant, even trivial, to the casual observer, but when employed on a systematic basis against a potential 'victim' the consequences can be devastating: deeply upsetting and humiliating. Nevertheless, because of the subtlety of the methods used, it's not hard to see why this area of bullying has been so difficult to define. How do we begin to distinguish teasing between friends from systematic attempts to 'diss' another person's integrity and self-respect? We need to move beyond this confusion if we're going to create some sensible strategies for real change, however. As long as this confusion continues, any definition of what is acceptable and unacceptable behaviour for girls will continue to remain blurred.

It is this blurring that allows the antisocial alpha female to dominate, while the victims are left to suffer in silence. As long as we only look for physical injury as proof of bullying we will not even begin to tackle the much more complex and subtle issues of girl bullying. We have to understand and acknowledge the complexities of psychological intimidation and the long-term consequences of humiliation and social exclusion. These indirect forms of harassment hide in the crevices of social structures. We barely begin to capture their essence in our current policies or practice.

As things stand, muddled thinking among adults, many of them in positions of responsibility, filters down to young people. As a result young people are confused about what does or does not constitute acceptable behaviour. This lack of clarity creates a vacuum. This vacuum creates inertia among those whose job it is to take action; it creates confusion among those who might report what they see if they had clearer guidelines to act on; and most of all feeds into the power of the antisocial alpha female to carry on as usual.

It is surely time to bite the bullet and commit ourselves to generating a practical, realistic and shared definition of bullying so that we can intervene with purpose and clarity; so that we can transform unhealthy antisocial behaviours into healthy pro-social behaviours for the good of individuals, education and society as a whole. But first we need to consider a few salient factors.

GENDER DIVIDE: SUGAR AND SPICE

Let's start with the traditional concept of bullying: the bigger, stronger pupil physically bullying a smaller, weaker one. It is not only boys who engage in this kind of aggression; girls do it too. They can fight just like boys – push and shove, poke, slap and thump just as malevolently. With physical bullying size matters: the bigger you are, the more likely you are to impose yourself. And while there are girls who bully physically, that should not deflect us from recognising the huge difference in the style of bullying that is embedded across the gender divide. Of course, girl bullies are constantly scanning for signs of weakness, but rather than scanning for physical size, girl bullies tend to scan for weakness in social status, and thus vulnerability to manipulation. In this lies the crucial difference between girl bullying and physical bullying. Whereas physical size is relatively stable, social status is constantly renegotiable. Retaining your place in a female social hierarchy is a relentless ongoing battle.

Gaining and maintaining a prominent position in the social structure is one of the key drivers for girl bullying. It is therefore essential that we include social manipulation in any definition of indirect bullying. When I asked girls aged between eight and fifteen whether there was any difference between how boys and girls tended to bully, over 90% described girl bullying as falling into three main categories: verbal intimidation, hostile body language and social aggression. Social aggression includes the manipulation of friendships and friendship groups. These are some typical responses:

> Girls bully by saying mean words, and boys bully by hurting each other.
>
> Zoe, aged 11

> They talk about you behind your back, steal your friends away until you're isolated and feel like crap all of the time.
>
> Becky, aged 13

> [They're] more vicious with their words and playing mind games, pretending to be your friend.
>
> Mia, aged 15

These girls recognise the wide variety of tactics that bullies use, from direct experience, and bluntly capture the essence of the gender divide. We need to start listening to them. They are clearly signposting that indirect bullying goes far deeper than the way it is usually described – *verbal bullying*. The term 'verbal bullying' is far too simplistic. It reduces indirect bullying, a central part of girl bullying, to being little more than nasty words. The result of such

simplification is that it normalises other manipulative and anti-social behaviours that the category 'verbal' doesn't capture. We need instead to see verbal bullying as only one part of indirect bullying, not all of it. We need to explore further to discover other themes that will create a more realistic and workable definition.

RELATIONAL AGGRESSION

I very much doubt it's news to anyone that antisocial alpha females use indirect methods to intimidate, but what precisely are those methods? Another big difference between boy bullying and girl bullying is what goes under the name of *relational aggression*. This is not a new term; in fact, it's been around for many years. Relational aggression is behaviour that is intended to hurt someone by intentionally harming their relationships with others or by diminishing their social status. We can see straight away how this is relevant to indirect bullying, and to girl bullying in particular, through tactics such as social isolation.

Playground culture is built around social games played with and through 'friendships'. The rules of these games are based on the very real and human need we have to build strong relationships and a sense of belonging. But once again, because taken alone the concepts of stealing friends, pretending to be a friends and falling out can seem – on the surface – to be temporary and trivial, it encourages those observers who are unprepared to look below the surface to claim, 'That's not bullying'. Sometimes, of course, there is nothing sinister when girls fall out. But to assume there is *never* anything sinister would be a huge mistake. Girl bullying is *all about the manipulation of friendships*. It's about using and abusing 'friendship' to hurt and control others.

Once we've got our heads around what relational aggression is and the damage it can cause, we can start to look out for it in the playground and elsewhere with a keener eye. When we're clear about which behaviours support the development of true friendship and which behaviours do not, it gets a lot easier to cut through the fog of loose definition and lazy observation. We can begin to recognise that teasing and falling out between friends is usually perfectly normal and signals nothing more than a realignment of that friendship. Teasing doesn't have a malicious intent to hurt or humiliate. Falling out is not about an imbalance of power; usually, it's just a difference of perspective.

So it's at this point that we need to draw a line between what constitutes issues in a friendship and what constitutes relational aggression. We could say that factors such as teasing and falling out are temporary phases in which a friendship is realigned or let go of in a normal and natural way, without malice. On the other hand, relational aggression abuses power and creates unhealthy interactions deliberately designed to make another suffer. We need to be clear about what are acceptable behaviours and what are unacceptable behaviours when dealing with these two separate aspects of relationships.

'FEELING LIKE CRAP ALL OF THE TIME'

One of the major problems in the UK, in my opinion, is that our approach is too rational. We tend to create definitions from a policy perspective. Such definitions do mention factors such as social isolation and friendship issues, but hardly ever acknowledge the really damaging *affective* factors, such as how bullying makes the victim feel. Policy descriptions can include acknowledgement that one person can hurt another physically or emotionally, but rarely seek to explain how this is done or what exactly are the unacceptable behaviours that lead to emotional distress.

While this lack of clarity and rigour pervades documentation and guidelines, vulnerable students will continue to suffer. As Becky says in the quote above, bullying made her 'feel like crap all of the time'. But she felt there was no point in reporting it because she'd come to believe feelings didn't count; that her feelings somehow weren't part of the direct evidence that she was being bullied.

Any type of bullying is likely to make a victim feel low, isolated and humiliated. And while not all young people will suffer long-term effects from bullying, the plain fact is that many victims who are psychologically humiliated and socially isolated do go on to suffer damage in their adult life, particularly around relationship and self-worth issues. For this reason alone, it is important that we include these affective factors in our definition of bullying. We should also recognise that bullies are susceptible to psychological damage too. While they possess one type of empathy which allows them to think about how their actions make others feel (*cognitive empathy*) they lack the ability to *feel* how others feel (*affective empathy*). They suffer from a lack of feeling in their unilateral desire for power and control over others. According to research (Jiang et al., 2011), many bullies develop patterns in childhood that may well lead them towards antisocial tendencies in their adult lives, and even criminal behaviour.

CYBERBULLYING

Research remains divided as to whether or not girls engage in cyberbullying more than boys do. What is clear, though, is that cyberbullying which seeks to put others down through attacking social status and relationships is mainly the province of girl bullying. In my discussion and focus groups with girls, on-screen social 'dissing' and character assassination is always a hot topic. They frequently say it's commonplace to 'diss' people on their Facebook page and then 'everyone just joins in'. What is eye-opening and somewhat alarming is the fact that this behaviour isn't seen by them as bullying, but as acceptable behaviour. In fact, these girls said they saw this as *expected* behaviour. If we are to come up with a useful new definition of bullying, we will need to take the vindictive antisocial element of girl bullying into account.

IT'S NOT BULLYING, IT'S THEIR FAULT!

Bullying is behaviour by an individual or group, repeated over time, that intentionally hurts another individual or group either physically or emotionally.

(DfE, 2014a, p. 6)

As we've already discussed, emotional hurt is difficult to pin down. The definition needs to be more evidence-based than it is in the DfE guidelines. In 1993, Dan Olweus wrote that in Scandinavia the word used for bullying is 'mobbing', which covers all forms of bullying: the pack, or mob, acting against the victim. Perhaps this idea could be a way to develop a greater understanding of girl bullying. What would socio-emotional mobbing look, sound and feel like?

In 2014, a report by Ofsted, the UK government's inspectorate for schools, made it clear that bullying was now considered to be a safeguarding issue, and recognised the importance of protecting vulnerable pupils from physical and emotional harm. But once again fine words are not enough to stop what is actually going on. If we're going to work out how to protect young people we need to find out what their attitudes and behaviours actually are. And if we take time to really listen to young people and the excuses they use to justify bullying, we can learn so much more about what the problem really is. When we do this, what immediately becomes clear is that there is no shared understanding of what bullying is – or is not.

I can be a bit intimidating – that's not bullying.

Cara, aged 15

Sometimes people bring it on themselves. If they say something to my face to annoy me then I'll get … It's not bullying, it's their fault.

Serena, aged 13

I wouldn't say it's bullying but I'd say I've been hard to people. Bullying is a constant thing you do over and over again. Being harsh is just people that annoy you.

Nina, aged 15

There are two immediately identifiable reasons why these young people fail to acknowledge their bullying behaviours. First, the current official definitions are just too ambiguous. Second, adults are failing to enforce models of what is and is not acceptable behaviour, often because they are confused themselves. While this situation continues, the pack or the mob will continue to excuse and justify their actions and behaviours as 'normal' and therefore perfectly acceptable.

The UK police have a motto – *Notice, Check, Share!* – which they use to alert children and adults alike to antisocial behaviour in order to minimise or prevent it. The idea is to promote awareness of unacceptable or threatening behaviour, thereby increasing the likelihood that people will report it. But what happens when a young person doesn't know or recognise that she or others are acting in an antisocial way? What happens when she sees adults behaving in similar ways, or adults not challenging acts of intimidation or social exclusion? What happens when TV and the media feed young people a constant diet of programmes that turn bullies into minor celebrities? If we're going to turn the tide we'll need to tighten our definitions of what is expected and acceptable behaviour and what is unacceptable. We need to actively promote, model and enforce what we might call *pro-social behaviours*.

THE ROLE OF POWER

Social power lies at the heart of girl bullying. Of course, power and status transactions are going on all the time in relationships, but what concerns us here is when social power is used in an unhealthy, abusive and antisocial way.

Some young children have a natural inclination towards leadership and some towards followership. And both roles are, of course, perfectly acceptable. Some children will find they are leaders in some groups, while in other groups they have much less power and influence. And that's perfectly normal too.

Let's imagine a little girl who exhibits leadership skills at an early age. For example, she might be bossy, constantly telling those in her group which games they should play and how they should play them. But the question is, how will those leadership skills play out? If she has parents or carers in her life who provide positive role models, who show pro-social, authoritative parenting skills in a safe and loving way, the chances are that she will develop into a pro-social alpha female, using her skills to benefit the people around her.

But other youngsters, those whose parents or carers offer little or no guidance in what constitutes skilful social behaviour, may not turn out to be quite so pro-social. They may well discover strategies that keep them protected, admired and dominant but which display a far less healthy style of leadership. Very often they will either have stumbled upon these strategies in the vacuum created by the lack of clear guidelines or learned them from others who manipulate power to get their way. Too often these people are parents, carers and sometimes even teachers. It is unfortunate that many schools cling to an authoritarian top-down structure that offers little room for the inclusion of students in policy-making and decision-making, especially in matters that directly concern them and in which they have much more experiential knowledge than the teachers themselves. Such hierarchical models can only reinforce the manipulative power hierarchies of the playground.

Even where student councils exist, too often they are selected from star pupils rather than those directly involved in bullying or being bullied so they are not representative. Too often student councils do not work for the general population of students.

Bearing all this in mind, we can say that the manipulative or abusive use of power needs to be considered in any useful definition of bullying. Alpha female bullies want to hold on to their power at all costs. They're addicted to it; it's what gives them status and protects them against others seeing their vulnerability and low self-image. When threatened they'll feign innocence and say any problem is the fault of the very people they're bullying. And as for the victims, they're too often left feeling invisible and isolated. As ten-year-old

Lucy says: 'You're nobody; no one cares about you ... everybody hates you ... they try and take over your life.'

SUMMARY

In this chapter we've considered the many reasons why finding a good working definition of bullying – in particular, indirect bullying – has been so difficult to establish. I've suggested that the key factors we need to consider are:

- Physical and psychological intimidation.

- Social manipulation and relational aggression, including:

    > Subtle and disrespectful verbal and non-verbal signals.

    > Humiliation.

    > Harassment.

    > Character assassination.

    > Vindictiveness.

    > Social exclusion.

- The short- and longer-term negative impact bullying can have on the feelings, sense of self-worth and social relationships of the victims.

Taking all these factors into consideration, here's a definition I'd like to suggest that enables us to move forward into theory, policy, practice and implementation with greater clarity. It allows us to form the basis of a practical set of guidelines that alert us to what may be going on in the playground and in cyberspace so that we – including the children themselves – can take timely action to intervene and create sustainable change. At the same time, it also allows us to begin a process of sensitising and educating young people to do the same by focusing on what are and are not acceptable social behaviours.

> Bullying consists of a complex web of antisocial behaviours that not only include physical intimidation but also verbal harassment, belittling verbal and non-verbal signals, the abuse of power, aggressive actions, the aggressive manipulation of friendships and the deliberate intention to cause a victim to feel distressed, humiliated or socially isolated.

Chapter 3

THE SOCIAL DEVELOPMENT OF GIRLS: HOW DO I LOOK IN YOUR EYES?

INTRODUCTION

In this chapter I'll sketch out the consequences that girl bullying can have on a young person's social development and self-esteem. In order to achieve a well-balanced sense of self, a child's social and emotional development needs to be nurtured with care. With appropriate attention and support, the child will learn to walk a developmental pathway that leads to secure attachments, trust and healthy relationships. But whenever a child becomes entangled in bullying, whether as the perpetrator or the victim, healthy development is likely to suffer: attachments, trust and relationships may well become viewed with suspicion and distrust.

So in this chapter I want to consider these questions: what role does social development play? And why is it so important for understanding how girl bullying works? I'll begin by exploring the notion of *sense of self*, especially in relation to how that develops throughout childhood. I'll also explore how social interactions and different types of friendship evolve, and the vitally important role these play in a child's development.

In order to look more closely into these issues, we'll need to disengage from the commonly held but simplistic notions that bullying has anything to do with innate temperament or personal traits, or that it is about apportioning fault and blame. It's far more useful instead to focus on the social roles played within the context of girl bullying. Finally, we will also need to distance ourselves from the idea that bullies lack social skill because in girl bullying that simply isn't true. In fact, the opposite is true. Girl bullies require sophisticated social skills in order to become the highly skilful manipulators they are.

Throughout childhood, social interactions help children learn how to fit into a wide variety of social settings. They have to work out what is expected, what is and is not acceptable behaviour and identify the rules for social interaction. They are on a steep learning curve to discover how relationships work and what they are all about. As children grow up, the social connections and relationships they develop and attempt to maintain help them define who they are in relation to 'others'. They learn to become aware of the ways that others see them and how they see themselves. A key element of this includes learning about friendships: how they work, why they work and how they sometimes go wrong. These lessons begin very early in a child's life, and in many ways it will be a lifelong journey of working through life's social hurts and disappointments. However, the ability to forge new relationships can be very seriously damaged when children experience deliberately targeted, unhealthy social interactions – bullying, in particular – on a regular basis during their childhood.

Children have to learn how to make friends, how to keep them and how to cope with the hurt and disappointment when friendships end. When children are not given the chance to learn these skills in a healthy way, their understanding of what a friendship is can become twisted. And as that twist tightens, the idea of who they are and how others see them can get tangled and distorted too.

Children and young people have to learn many rules of social engagement. They learn what they can and can't do, how to get hugs, how to talk and how to play. If all goes well, they learn how to negotiate the trials and tribulations of social interaction across many different contexts. A child will experience numerous types of social interaction on their journey from babyhood to adulthood. And that pathway can sometimes be a minefield; relationships always contain an element of risk as we make ourselves vulnerable to those we reach out to. One step in the wrong direction and a child's growing, fragile self could be in jeopardy. When a child's openness and vulnerability are exploited and manipulated by a person or group who deliberately want to humiliate or exclude them from the social circle, it's not unusual for that child to feel that their world is caving in. When such a crisis happens, they are forced to ask themselves: *who am I, and how do others see me?*

TODDLERS TO TEENS: THE EMERGING SENSE OF SELF

Children really don't have much of a choice about the how, where and why of their social development in the early and formative stages of their lives. It's down to others: parents, grandparents, carers and, later on, teachers. It's their rules, their lessons and their examples that will strongly influence and shape each child's sense of self. The social lessons children learn from adults will influence them both at home and school, and, later in life, will still exert some impact over their relationships at work and in their adult social interactions. These adults will inevitably be drawn from the ranks of the good, the bad and the ugly. Some will be wonderful, attentive parents and carers, while others may not give a damn. A child's sense of self is hugely impacted by the way the child feels 'seen' and how she is treated and valued. The simple fact is that, in the early stages of child development, the quality of parenting, caring or safeguarding can develop the confidence of a child – or destroy it.

I've seen the long-term effects of poor, and even bullying, guardianship too often in my behaviour clinics: adult women psychologically damaged by the impact of persistent negative social interactions during their childhood. They sit opposite me, talking through their problems, until eventually the psychological scars of their early years become visible.

Very often these women's confidence was seriously knocked during their early years, and this left them vulnerable to bullying: girl bullies tend to be expert at scanning for signs of weakness, such as low self-esteem and low self-confidence. Some of the adult women I see can't accept a compliment. They can't bear to look in the mirror or see their reflection in a shop window because it reminds them of their sense of worthlessness. It may even remind them of the times they were bullied, bringing back the sound, actions and the power of the bully, and their own deep sense of fear and self-loathing. Their view of self has been so deeply damaged that five, ten, fifteen, twenty years later these others still haunt them and, in a deep psychological way, continue to dominate their lives. The impact of bullying can be soul-destroying. In many ways it's a wonder that more girls and women don't resort to suicide. Thank goodness they don't.

In order to understand this situation better, let's take a deeper look at the notion of 'self'. The concept of self can be separated into three elements: self-awareness, self-concept and self-esteem.

- Self-awareness begins when the child realises that she is a being, distinct and separate from others. She begins to develop and form a conscious knowledge of her own character, feelings, motives and desires.

- Self-concept is an idea of the self that is constructed both from the beliefs a child holds about herself and from the responses of others: I am kind; I am honest; I am naughty; I am a pain in the backside.

- Self-esteem reflects the confidence a child has in her own worth or abilities from her own perspective or through the eyes of others: how good am I? How good am I in your eyes? How worthy am I? How worthy am I in your eyes?

Let's start where the sense of self begins. A young baby has no idea where her physical self starts and ends. She'll startle as her own hand appears in front of her face. But in the first eight weeks of life, she'll learn that these little hands are her own and she'll slowly realise where her physical self begins and ends. This mapping of her physical geography is neurological, a result of cognitive processing. She thinks her way into the map and then remembers it. The same process occurs with social maps, but unfortunately without the simplicity and speed that the physical body map offers.

During the first twelve months of life, a baby begins to stumble through the complicated process of communicating her needs to others and interacting with them in a way that – all being well – keeps her safe and loved. By the age of two she'll be able to communicate with a few words, a great deal of body language and some very clever emotional manipulation of those around her. She'll not only get her needs met but her wants as well. By three she'll have developed some really effective and subtle methods of social interaction that help her get a sense of who she is. Her personality is forming, as this grandmother found out:

> Meme, you got purse?
> Yes.
> Meme, you money in there?
> Yes.
> Oh. Me want Kinder 'prise egg.

Meme gives her a look that says 'you little monkey', but she simply can't say no. She's caught by the subtle interaction methods – and the little one knows it. And with all of the knowledge that I have of children and their tactics, I have to admit to you that I'm that grandma, and I fall into the trap every time! Little children can engineer social interactions brilliantly. Their sense of self has emerged, and they've come to realise that they're an individual with their own needs and desires, and separate from the adults around them. Their *self-concept* is fed by the reactions of those around them. The 'little monkey' look tells my granddaughter that she's very cheeky, and the 'reward' of getting the chocolate lets her know that she's just a little bit smart. Similarly, if the child's self-esteem has also been nourished with praise, kindness and affection, it will make the child feel worthy.

Positive social interactions such as these lay the foundations for healthy social and emotional development. Children learn the social rules and discover how to engage with others – until the time comes for them to attend nursery school … and everything they have learned so far is thrown into chaos and confusion as new sets of social rules, interactions and social hierarchies come in to play.

The ideas of self, so painstakingly established at home, will be challenged in the bigger arena of school. Codes of interactions now revolve around play: which toys can the child play with without upsetting other little boys and girls? How does the child learn to play games with others that she doesn't know? How does the child find her place in a large group? The child's idea of self has to adapt rapidly. She has to learn new skills very quickly to fit in as the social roles of leaders, followers and bystanders inevitably emerge among a room full of three- to five-year-olds. As the self-concept and self-esteem of each child is challenged and confronted by the needs and wishes of others, tears, tantrums and fisticuffs are not uncommon.

Conflict and confusion are inevitable as children battle for roles and figure out where they fit in. And what happens in the nursery school – the jockeying for position, status and inclusion – in many ways foreshadows what will happen in the secondary school playground some eight or nine years in the future. In certain social groups the leaders will continue to lead, the followers to follow and the challengers to challenge. And while most will also learn to swap and adapt these roles in different social settings, others will not be able to be so flexible. But for now it's more benign. Leaders, followers and bystanders are all mixed together and boys and girls relatively easily mingle together. Boys and girls play together, fight together, scowl at each other and begin to hug and help each other.

Things begin to change around the age of six. Gender differences start to emerge in play and socialising. Soon these differences will dominate playground dynamics. Girls play with girls, boys with boys. As larger numbers of children are corralled together at primary school, 'leaders' begin to emerge and play a more dominant role. Those who need to, and are able to, attempt to build up their social self and status, becoming stronger in whatever ways they can. For boys it's often based on physical size or social 'cool'. For girls it's different. It's all about who is most socially popular.

By the age of nine or ten, girls begin to build relationships based on something more in-depth than sameness or similarity. They cement their newly forming friendships by sharing secrets and personal information. Friendship is all about sharing and owning each other's intimate details. As ten-year-old Tia wrote about the qualities of her best friends: 'you can rely on them to keep a secret'.

Perhaps it's worth noting that this sharing of intimate details and personal information is a trait that will differentiate most women from most men for the rest of their lives. Wanting to know intimate details and personal information in order to cement a relationship is not only something little girls do – big girls do it too. Imagine two married couples, who know each other well, on a night out. At some stage they split up and have separate conversations. The men will most likely stick to safe subjects that don't carry much emotional content. They might talk about sport, work or their interests. The two women, meanwhile, will very likely have been trading reciprocal secrets and personal information. It's a form of social security without a cheque. The payment they get instead is perceived affiliation based on these shared secrets. When I polled girls' views about what made someone a good friend, forty out of forty-seven of them said trust, loyalty and the ability to keep secrets.

There is one more key element I need to mention, and that is the social judgements that decide who's in and who's out of a group. By the age of ten, positive and negative labels are used and readily attached to peers. 'I am better than you' is a common judgement about self. 'You aren't good enough to be my friend' is a common judgement about others. In the cut and thrust of the playground, where social connections are constantly being made and unmade, assessments like these can all too easily damage a fragile sense of self and self-concept, chipping away at self-esteem. When a child comes to believe that they are who the other children have said they are, the damage can filter its way through to the very core of that child. If there is any sense of malice or manipulation involved, as is certainly the case with bullying, such judgements can cause the child's view of friendship to change, as well as how she perceives herself as a person and as a friend.

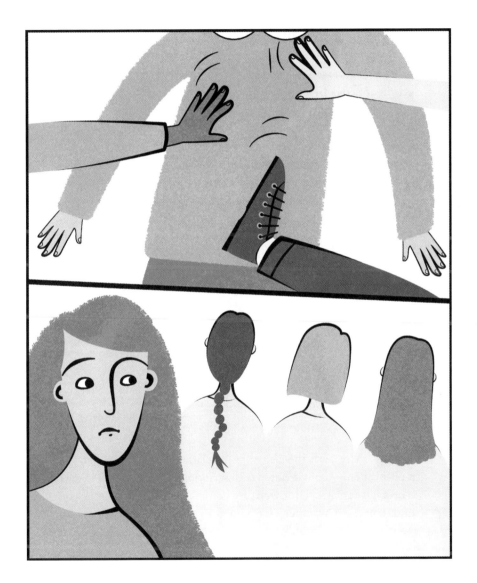

THE ROLE OF FRIENDSHIP: EXCLUSION/INCLUSION

By way of contrast, let's turn our attention now to the comfort and security offered by healthy friendships. Healthy friendships are supportive and nurturing. They have strong elements of mutuality, of give and take, reciprocal trust, respect and loyalty. A circle of friends that can be trusted, even if it's just one other person, is essential for developing a positive sense of self in the child, and also for developing a positive sense about how others see her as well. Healthy friendships reflect our ability to form positive, sustainable relationships that benefit the child and her friends. These relationships are based on shared likes and interests and offer a triple win: a win for the child, a win for the friends and – because these friendships are collaborative and nurturing – a win for the wider community. This is how two young people describe their idea of a good friend:

> Being kind, letting friends play, and staying friends forever.
>
> Lara, aged 9

> [They] don't slag you off, they're truthful, not two-faced, [they] always be with you.
>
> Hakima, aged 13

Contrast these with the elements of relational aggression that are implicit in ten-year-old Serena's description of what she considers to be a false friend. 'They won't let you play with your friends, you think you can trust them for something personal then [they] go and tell everyone.'

For most of us, loyalty and shared interests are an essential element of friendship for girls. But loyalty and shared goals are also to be found in unhealthy friendships. A girl bully and her 'pack' or 'mob' will meet some of the criteria that we've established for a healthy friendship. But the unhealthy aspects soon become clear when we start to examine what's going on more closely; in particular, when we start to consider the negative impact of the relationships within the pack on each girl's concept of self. In a pack, each girl's role is to show loyalty and deference to the bully, the alpha female. Each girl's sense of self can easily become a shadow of its potential. Self-concept and self-esteem become all too dependent on the mood of the alpha. To protect themselves from exclusion, each girl diminishes her own sense of self in order to identify more fully with the pack. The social need to be 'together forever' can seem attractive, even in this antisocial, twisted environment. And no matter how non-reciprocal, conflict-ridden or dominated those friendships might be, some young people need to know that they 'belong' somewhere, anywhere, rather than face the alternative of being cast out into the wilderness of social exclusion.

SUMMARY

What conclusions can we draw from the previous paragraphs? On the one hand, we can say that the ability to develop healthy friendships gives a child a strong sense of self, a place to rest and feel safe. True friends provide a sense of being wanted, of feeling safe and accepted. This also gives a child a sense of personality that others want to identify with. On the other hand, we see that while social identity can influence our self-concept for the better, it can also change it for the worse. In unhealthy relationships, children can be influenced to give up their sense of identity, becoming the 'puppet' of a child with a stronger personality. Their desire to be 'seen' and included in the social group can skew their sense of right and wrong. As the child's concept of who she is becomes embedded in someone else's identity, her self-esteem plummets. This does not happen in a healthy friendship.

There is one more important point to consider here. Friendship, whether healthy or not, teaches young people how social support works. When the relationships are healthy, the support works very well. We know that children who have healthy friendships are more socially competent than those who do not. But when the relationships are unhealthy, life can be made very uncomfortable indeed for some young people; for others, life can become unbearable and not worth living.

We need to be very clear about this. Unhealthy friendships are deviant, cause long-term damage to self-esteem and self-concept, and seriously threaten healthy social development. We also need to acknowledge the benefit of belonging and the impact that social exclusion has on a young person's sense of self. But now that we're aware of the benefits and risks to social development that healthy and unhealthy friendships offer, and the part that social exclusion can play within those friendships, we are in a much better position to develop the beginnings of a strategy that will help us to deal with girl bullying.

Chapter 4

THE CULTURAL VACUUM: THE FACTORS THAT CREATE CONDITIONS FOR BULLYING, AND WHY SO MUCH MORE NEEDS TO BE DONE

INTRODUCTION

In the previous chapter we explored how self-esteem and self-concept are shaped as a child's social world grows. Now let's turn our attention to the role that culture plays in creating and maintaining the conditions in which girl bullying thrives. In order to do this, we'll need to explore three key areas: *dispositional* factors, *situational* factors and *systemic* factors.

Dispositional factors are the innate traits that mark an individual's general character, such as being kind, generous, aggressive or mischievous. Situational factors occur when a child experiences a specific context or environment that strongly influences them, for better or worse. For example, an acrimonious relationship between his parents might cause a child to become stressed and behave aggressively; or continual harassment from other children might cause a child, in the heat of the moment, to react in a violent or spiteful way. Systemic factors are more embedded over time and context. They occur in stable and dominant systems such as schools, extended families, social institutions (such as youth clubs, Guides and Scouts), and across the media, including TV and the internet. These dominant cultures reinforce certain attitudes and behaviours as acceptable and normal. The values embedded in these systems typically have a powerful influence over a child's thinking and behaviours.

Looking more closely at these three areas, and the interrelationships between them, will help us as we begin to unravel the factors and cultural contexts that shape young people's thinking and attitudes. It's vitally important that we take this wider perspective, because bullying is a learned behaviour. It's an interaction caused by the interplay between each of these three factors.

Once we've explored the impact these settings and influences can have on young people, we'll have a 'bigger picture' awareness of the contexts that create the conditions in which bullying develops and is able to thrive. We'll also have a better understanding of the challenges that need to be addressed, and what has to happen if we are to change the all too common responses to bullying of acceptance and apathy.

DISPOSITIONAL FACTORS

Let's start by considering the role played by dispositional factors, and the danger of paying attention only to these when we wish to challenge and change bullying behaviours and bullying cultures. Too often, in the past, adults have looked to pin the blame on individuals: either the bullies themselves or, in some cases, their victims. But we have to ask ourselves, is there really such a thing as a born intimidator or a natural born victim? In my view, it's most unlikely. As I explore in this chapter, girl bullying is caused by many factors.

What this means is that it's not enough to only consider a handful of dominant personality traits as being sufficient to create a bully or a culture in which bullying can thrive. We need to consider other factors that contribute to this problem.

In this chapter I want to tease out some of these issues from the shadows. But in order to do this, I first have to set aside the tendency to jump too quickly to judgement. We need to avoid using easy and simplistic labels such as 'bad', 'evil', 'weak' or 'born victim'. We need to get away from looking only at the dispositional factors so that we can take a judicious step back and engage with the bigger picture. It's a mistake to think that bullying occurs on the spur of the moment. The reality is that it's an end point of a long, and often bruising, social journey.

If only it were possible to put bullying down to fixed dispositional traits alone. We would be able to identify bullies in primary school, at nursery, in the home, in the pram! It would be convenient, but not very helpful. The fact is that life doesn't work like that. People change; disposition and temperament aren't as fixed as many would like to think. In fact, it's quite common for victims to become bullies, and vice versa, depending on time and context. Fourteen-year-old Sheena reported to me that she'd suffered bullying at primary school and had learned to toughen up by the time she reached secondary school: 'I used to get bullied at primary school a bit. Now if someone says something to me I stick up for myself ... they'd walk over me if I didn't change.'

Sheena's story is not at all uncommon and directly challenges the tendency to label too quickly and too easily. One school might have labelled Sheena a victim; the other, a bully. This example illustrates my point that bullying behaviours are learned. They're learned for different reasons, including responding to what different situations require, copying or 'modelling' the behaviours of what works for others, and by adapting to the different cultural systems in which the child finds herself. Disposition and temperament do have a role to play, but perhaps not as much as some would have us believe.

It is far more useful to think about bullying in terms of what has caused the child to become a bully, a victim or a bystander rather than simply blaming them for it. This doesn't mean that children shouldn't take responsibility for their own actions; of course they should. But it also means that, as adults, it's more helpful if we take the trouble to look at the bigger picture. We need to engage our senses to pick up clues that will direct us to circumstances that are effecting changes in a child's behaviour. There will be a reason, per-haps several, for a child being aggressive, angry, shy or vulnerable; just as there will be reasons for a child being empathetic, resilient or caring. So when we notice a child's behaviour changing – becoming more stressed, for example, or more inattentive to schoolwork – we need to ask ourselves what might be going on.

If we notice a child become more socially dominant in a way we may suspect is not altogether healthy, we also need to ask ourselves what might be the reasons for this. We need to be vigilant and curious, to find out what's actually going on. What's happening at that child's home? Are the cultural norms of power, authority and inclusion that operate within the child's school, or at the social institutions to which the child belongs, healthy or unhealthy? And what's actu-ally happening in the playground? Are the children's activities and attitudes really as benign as they seem to be at first glance? Or can one spot, if one looks carefully enough, signs of threatening, intimidating, manipulative and exclusive behaviours – the early warning signs of bullying?

Of course individual traits, temperament and disposition do make a difference and we need to consider these within the contexts given above. Children are different from each other and their dispositional traits will play a significant role in how they respond to the different situations and systems they must operate within.

As an example, let's take resilience. Different children have different levels of resilience. Some of them bounce back from adversity and become stronger, while others are defeated and even destroyed by it. Bullying, and other stressful relationships or events, tend to bring these dispositional differences into sharper focus. Sheena, in the example above, felt she had become stronger through the experience of being bullied; so much so that she felt she could now try on the role of bully for herself when she reached secondary school. Yet in the Introduction, Jodie's story revealed how bullying had made her feel manipulated, isolated and worthless.

Thus, while we can say that dispositional traits can influence or even determine how children respond to the behaviour of others, this is always in the context of other factors, which are situational and systemic.

SITUATIONAL FACTORS

As the name suggests, situational factors arise out of particular moments in everyday contexts. The child's general experience of home may be that she is neglected by her parents or carers. She feels unseen, unappreciated or unworthy. It may be that one of her parents is an alcoholic, abusive or incredibly self-centred. If she is a girl, she may live in a household where she feels she is not given the same status as boys or where expectations of girls are generally lower. These are systemic factors and the child may have learned to cope with them. However, something may arise that triggers a strong reaction in the child, such as a particular incident, event or situation.

For example, the child arrives at school feeling raw thanks to the attitudes, treatment or situation she has experienced at home. She feels she's had enough; she's on the edge. And then she encounters a teacher who is just doing his job: stretching the students to achieve their potential by asking them to give a presentation or setting them a challenging test. But for the child, fresh from the negative experience at home, it can be the proverbial straw that breaks the camel's back. It's too much. She reacts – maybe not against the teacher, but later, in the playground, she vents her frustration and anger on another child; a child who may just be unlucky enough to get in her way at the wrong moment. She lashes out in the heat of the moment, and the damage is done. She's instantly labelled as a bully.

A one-off incident such as the above can trigger a pattern of reactive behaviour. It becomes an unhealthy coping strategy that the child uses to get through each day. School becomes the place where she deals with her problems. And sometimes there's something about school that allows her to do so, which allows her to play out her power games with an audience and very often to get away with it. It can be hard to put one's finger on exactly what is going on. But whatever it is, it's a complex mix of situational factors that give her the space and opportunity to act out her feelings and impose them on others.

These situational factors include the social hierarchy of the school playground, which can create a very fertile ground for girl bullying. In particular, this reflects the way that many girls tend to view social power, especially the way social power is deeply connected with popularity at school.

Duncan and Owens (2011) carried out extensive research into social popularity. They asked fourteen- to sixteen-year-old girls to rank statements such as 'takes drugs', 'comes from a tough family', 'is quite thin', 'is very loud', 'has been involved in scandal', 'is really pretty' and 'is very popular with boys' on grids that ranged from 'least popular' to 'most popular'. The girls then took part in a discussion about their choices and their attitudes towards concepts of peer popularity. The results showed that the 'most popular' girls were thought by peers to be 'attractive to boys' and 'mildly rebelliousness' at school. These were the girls considered to be the most valued, esteemed and powerful. The least popular girls were viewed as 'worthless', 'disrespected' and 'vulnerable'. This study provided a strong link between girls' popularity and how girl bullying is driven by perceptions of social power and social identity at school. It also reflects how being 'unpopular' and a victim of bullying made Jodie feel 'worthless', as she described herself in the Introduction.

Now let's consider what would happen if conditions conspire to make a child feel worthless at home *and* at school. There's a high chance that their self-esteem could be so low that they become a victim in both situations. On the other hand, the worthlessness they feel at home could trigger a reaction – a reactive behaviour against their sense of oppression or injustice. In this case they might seize the opportunity that the school environment affords, especially where adult vigilance and safeguarding procedures are lax, to reach for social power; to find a way to become popular through antisocial behaviour. Having observed how other girls use various strategies to be seen as popular and powerful, they might well decide to model their behaviours on what brings success to others. It might just be all they need to do, so their thinking goes, to acquire that much desired feeling of self-worth and admiration from others. At the very least, to feel worthy in just one situation, whether you achieve this by bullying or not, is better than never feeling worthy at all.

Of course, these unhealthy reactive behaviours are unacceptable, but when we take a step back and look at the underlying context we can at least begin to understand why they occur. We see the situational and systemic factors that create the potential for frustration, manipulation of others, anger and violence. Once we understand these better, we can begin to take action about how to work with and redress them. We can begin to look for strategies that will help the child to deal with her emotions more effectively, adapt to different situations more healthily and also try to handle the issues more skilfully at home. The following case study shows how systemic and situational factors create the conditions for antisocial behaviours to occur, and how the complex way the issues are interwoven can make it difficult for not just the observers but even the main actors to see what's really going on.

> Fourteen-year-old Jamie's case was typical of this pattern, but it took her months to understand why she did what she did. She needed time to calm down and reflect on what had happened, but by the time she'd done that she'd already got herself into serious trouble, not only in school but also with the law.
>
> Jamie had huge issues and an awful lot of stress at home. Her family problems had been evident for a long time. These issues had also affected her at school, where she'd become known and labelled as a bully. On the particular day in question, she'd had a lot of stress at home because of the actions of an older sibling: an allegation of assault.
>
> When Jamie arrived at school that morning, angry and frustrated, she snapped. As she told me later: 'This person annoyed me and I turned around and I hit her, like very hard, and I did damage … I regret it but then I think, yeah, she deserved it … if people egg you on and if you're like "no" [then] you're a pussy …'
>
> And after that she quietly added, 'But that day was like … such a hard day for me.'

This isn't a pretty tale, but it does show how different dispositional, situational and systemic factors come together to create and even reinforce the conditions in which bullying occurs.

SYSTEMIC FACTORS

Finally, let's look beyond the dispositional and situational factors to the systemic ones. Systemic factors are those that occur in the home, at school, in leisure contexts such as clubs and organisations, and in the media. These systemic contexts provide the cultural norms on which young people model their behaviours and develop their values and attitudes. But sometimes the norms that these contexts offer are not particularly healthy. Rather than offering models that promote inclusive, developmental and pro-social behaviours, some offer the opposite, while others turn a blind eye to abuses. At worst, some of these contexts actually glorify antisocial behaviours. Many reality TV shows, for example, actively seem to promote bad behaviour, including bullying.

Of course, it's people who make and create systems. The problem can be that sometimes systems take on a life of their own. And when this 'life' creates a culture that is antisocial, or even toxic, we have a big challenge on our hands. Psychologist Philip Zimbardo has explored this phenomenon. In his book, *The Lucifer Effect* (2007), he investigated how the abuse of prisoners in Abu Ghraib and other prisons in Iraq led to otherwise 'good' people behaving in appalling ways. He asked, what makes good people turn bad? Was it perhaps the stressful circumstances? Or maybe the culture introduced by senior military staff? He was particularly interested in how the term 'bad apple' had been used by the official investigators. According to Zimbardo, using that term allowed the authorities to shift blame away from the situations that occurred and the system in which they occurred – the US military – and towards the individual perpetrators of the abuse. Zimbardo, an emeritus professor of psychology at Stanford University in California, argued that while these individuals were not exempt from responsibility, it was the military top brass who had put the regime in place. They were the most culpable, by their failure to ensure that the prison was managed according to the norms of justice or the Geneva Convention. He concluded that pointing the finger of blame solely at the dispositional traits of individuals was not only wrong but missed the true cause of the evil. Zimbardo summed up his own research by making the point that it's not about a bad apple, but a 'bad barrel'. It was primarily a systemic problem. He called his theory about how easy it is for normal people to succumb to evil the 'The Lucifer Effect', after God's favourite angel who fell from grace and eventually became Satan.

Zimbardo's work is a useful analogy through which to consider why some otherwise well-balanced young people may turn to antisocial behaviours, including bullying. Young people too are embedded in systems. And it's up to the adults who are responsible for those systems to take frequent long, hard looks both at themselves and at the systems they put in place or manage, in order to check whether or not they themselves are part of the problem.

FUNCTIONAL AND DYSFUNCTIONAL SCHOOL SYSTEMS

Let's consider school systems. First, it's important to say that most schools operate perfectly well and some are exemplary. The best schools tend to work directly with pupils when writing anti-bullying policies, so pupils can create and own definitions of what bullying is and isn't, decide and impose sanctions and other consequences, and support the implementation of the chosen strategies. In these schools bullying is understood and taken seriously, and numerous reporting routes are offered. Both proactive and reactive strategies are implemented and regularly reviewed. Each case is taken on an individual basis, and each case is dealt with using a tailored approach, suitable for the individuals concerned. Such schools revisit their anti-bullying policies annually and ensure they are practically applicable and understood by all stakeholders: pupils, parents, school staff and governors. Sanctions are applied to all those found guilty of using bullying behaviours, but at the same time these schools ensure that they also offer support to all pupils involved, including bystanders.

When both students and parents are involved in policy-making, alongside staff, it has a huge beneficial impact. In the past, pupils and parents of some of these schools had either been unaware of the anti-bullying policies or they'd complained about anti-bullying policies being inaccessible and unreadable. In response, many of the schools concerned then redressed these issues by making an active effort to include pupils and parents in the writing and production of their policy, with great success.

However, there are some schools, including some schools in which I've worked, that don't come up to these high standards. In these schools girl bullying is frequently dismissed as just 'girls being girls'. Definitions, sanctions and strategies are conspicuously absent, as is any idea of the students themselves being included in the process. It's hardly surprising that in these situations bullying behaviours are rife, become all too easily normalised, and a culture of fear and manipulation pervades the playground. This is how a systemic culture of bullying begins, establishes itself and prospers, disregarded or at best unnoticed by those in 'authority'.

Modelling is a crucial part of this process. It's essential that teachers model pro-social behaviours such as respect, listening, enquiry and tolerance rather than their opposites. If teachers and staff don't set positive and powerful examples of expected behaviour, there's little hope that young children will develop them by themselves. For the sake of argument, let's consider what might happen in a notional school where the following problems occur. Perhaps a staff member uses bullying tactics to control children rather than more acceptable authoritative strategies to keep necessary order in a respectful way. For example, I was told about one primary teacher who threw a chair out of his classroom while screaming at his class. The children were terrified, but the teacher undoubtedly kept a form of 'control' over those children. The problem, of course, is that this kind of bullying behaviour, which instils fear in children, can easily become a model for some of them. They see that forceful, threatening and sometimes violent behaviour can help them get their way – and so they begin to copy it.

Another example in our notional school might be that some of the staff are seen to disrespect, or even use unilateral power over, other members of staff. Once again, when students see teachers behaving in this way, it's hardly surprising that some will come to the conclusion that it's OK to bully others in order to get their way. Those of us in positions of authority must get our own house in order before we can expect those in our care to improve their own behaviours.

When bullying behaviours and attitudes are tolerated among staff members, and go unaddressed, it's not difficult to see how easily a culture can arise where bullying isn't seen, isn't reported and isn't acted upon because it's experienced as normal and acceptable. In fact, in these dysfunctional cultures, it's not uncommon to find a school which has adopted a healthy anti-bullying policy on paper but then finds the policy is unenforceable because most of the anti-social behaviours that constitute bullying are seen as acceptable and normal in the day-to-day life of the school. Just as in Abu Ghraib.

THE MEDIA: FILMS, TV AND THE INTERNET

When considering unhealthy systemic factors that feed into the rise and embedding of antisocial behaviours in young people and teenagers, it's impossible to ignore the role that the media plays, both on the big screen (film and TV) and on the small screen (computers, tablets and mobile phones). Film and TV offer a staple diet these days of antisocial behaviour dressed up as family entertainment. Shows such as *Gossip Girl*, films such as *Mean Girls* and *The Duff* and reality TV programmes such as *Dance Moms* all promote indirect bullying behaviours in one way or another. These bullying behaviours include harassment, abuses of power and ritual humiliation. It has all become depressingly normal.

It's not hard to see how the 'celebrity style' girl bully, who becomes popular through social power in the form of being adored and admired, might crave that particular kind of social identity. And it's not hard to see either why those around her want to reinforce it and be close to her. These TV programmes promote minor celebrities to achieve fame – or perhaps I should say notoriety – not through talent or hard work but through antisocial and bullying behaviours. In turn, these 'non-ebrities', as someone once memorably described them, whose bad behaviours, messy private lives and wealth are reported daily in the tabloids and elsewhere, become unhealthy role models for impressionable young people to copy. Fifteen-year-old Chelsea told me how she feels about these celebrities and their antisocial antics: 'thing is, everyone likes watching them; that's why they're so popular, like; you can say that you don't, but everyone likes watching them 'cause it's excitement'.

Another powerful driver of antisocial behaviours in young people are leisure activities, where healthy and unhealthy systems and hierarchies operate in just the same way. A few years ago I was asked to work with the England Rugby Football Union devising anti-bullying workshops for young rugby players after a focus on safeguarding issues was highlighted among amateur youth teams, both in their games and in training. The only way I could think of to tackle bullying issues in this context was to use the language and culture of the game itself to help these young men see what bullying is and why sanctions needed to be put in place. I worked

from the basis of their safeguarding policy and the way players 'look after' their team-mates during matches. I also imported some of the sanctions used by youth teams on the rugby field for foul play: for example, a free kick for a less serious infringement and a penalty for a more serious foul. In some junior games, the distance to the goal posts from which penalties are taken varies for different degrees of foul play. The workshops were developed around themes that were understood in the sport, such as playing hard and fair, but also within the rules of a sport that has an essential element of power and brute force.

The last case history I want to share in this chapter is one that suggests that, if we are not vigilant, systemic bullying can show up in the most surprising places. One might think that the Girl Guides movement is an incredibly pro-social group – and, of course, it generally is. But there are always exceptions. Dominique told me about her experience with the Guides in a north-western European country. And what makes this example particularly shocking is that the bullying was carried out and supervised not by young people but by those in authority: the leaders.

> Scouts and Guides have a tradition known as totemisation. [It starts with a ritual] during which each individual is given the name of an animal that is said to resemble them [in some way]. My own experience of totemisation [was] when I was twelve ... [At the campsite] we were made to perform a variety of humiliating acts, such as throwing ourselves on the ground while wailing, having (fake) poo shoved into our mouths and given riddles that in a normal setting would be very easy to solve, but became impossible under that amount of pressure. Many girls, including myself, simply shut down completely. Another girl was given the totem Beluga [white whale] which was

unfortunate because of her size and weight. I'm sure this didn't help her self-image and the anorexia she later developed.

Of course, many Guides and Scouts love the rough and tumble of camping and the traditional rituals that have taken place at these events for many years. Nevertheless, sometimes things can get out of hand. Not everyone appreciates the physical aspects of these kinds of initiations, and vigilance needs to be exercised so that potentially traumatising activities are excluded. At the very least, perhaps, some of the more traditional initiation ceremonies could be adapted to more enlightened ones that don't rely on physical or psychological intimidation.

SUMMARY

In this chapter I've looked at the roles played by dispositional, situational and systemic factors in the development of bullying behaviours and the conditions in which bullying can easily flourish. These factors – some healthy, some unhealthy, depending on context – influence the many ways young people develop their social attitudes and values. Depending on the level and quality of guidance from adults, especially those in positions of social influence, these factors can lead to either pro-social or antisocial behaviours.

Bullying thrives in contexts where highly regarded antisocial behaviours can be modelled and enacted without sanctions because the dominant culture has accepted them as the norm. Many TV programmes, internet dissing, dysfunctional family relationships, low quality vigilance and monitoring in schools, and the playground culture of 'top dog' and 'Miss Popular' all feed into the creation of cultures and environments where manipulative bullying behaviours and unhealthy coping strategies go ignored or unrecognised. Only when we have begun to acknowledge, recognise and admit the part we ourselves have played as adults in the interrelationship between these factors can we begin to develop an effective suite of proactive and reactive anti-bullying approaches.

While it is true that we cannot change all the factors that directly influence children today, we can at least focus on those that are within our direct sphere of influence: youth clubs, activity, leisure and sports clubs, and most of all schools. If we begin to take well-thought-out action to create healthier cultures and social attitudes in these environments, and actively encourage more pro-social behaviours among young people, perhaps from there we can start to build a more robust foundation and scaffolding from which to challenge the less than healthy values and attitudes that pervade and are so mindlessly promoted in the media.

Bullying will always exist to some extent because it is in the nature of human beings to test for power and social status. This jockeying for position is a natural part of development and can be healthy or unhealthy. Changing the attitudes and behaviours of those young people who, for whatever reasons, find it easier to take the less healthy and more antisocial routes will likely be more of a challenge.

Usually, it's not just a matter of their disposition or temperament, but of the wider situational and systemic influences that impact upon them: their experiences of, and reactions to, the world around them. Whatever the case, they find bullying behaviour is, for them, an effective coping strategy. With this in mind, every responsible adult, and even every responsible child, can benefit from collab-oratively devising anti-bullying approaches, strategies and policies that allow everyone who is impacted in any way by bullying to be involved and engaged in its eradication or, at the very least, its diminution.

Chapter 5

THE MAKING OF THE WOLF PACK

INTRODUCTION

So far I have explored how the historic lack of clear definitions, the general social development of girls and the absence of healthy cultural norms in many social and institutional contexts have combined to create the ideal conditions for girl bullying not only to remain largely unchallenged, but also to thrive. Let's now take a look at what happens when all of those factors come together and girl bullying takes its most aggressive form: the wolf pack led by the alpha female. We'll consider the qualities of the alpha female, how the pack is selected and formed, and how factors such as bystander apathy and the unwillingness of individuals to take responsibility for reporting aggressive or malicious incidents, all keep bullying continuing.

THE ALPHA FEMALE:
A LUMINOUS BEACON WITH A DARK SIDE

An alpha female is no bad thing. At least, not when she operates in a pro-social way. She's a leader, a strong willed decision-maker, an independent thinker and a role model. She can provide strength and stability to those who choose to be around her. She's focused, tenacious and aims for success. And she'll often have an acute sense of emotional intelligence, tuning in to the emotional needs of others as well as herself.

But what happens when an alpha female decides to use these skills and qualities for antisocial purposes? When she chooses to advance her own needs at the expense of others, to manipulate and bully her 'friends' within the pack and her victims beyond it? What happens when the alpha female slips over to the dark side?

In my experience, the most prevalent type of alpha female is the 'celebrity' bully. She is normally good at something – whether it's decision-making, sporting achievement, academic prowess, or simply being good-looking and utilising those looks. She holds court in the playground. And let's make her real. We'll call her Alpha. There is an Alpha in most schools. She likes to be noticed. There's nothing wrong with that. She likes attention. There's nothing wrong with that either. And she can also morph into other roles, either aggressive or passive, depending on the space and place. That's not unusual. Sometimes in the park – without her pack around her – she'll be a victim, or in a leisure club she'll be a bystander. But in other contexts she's the alpha. It all depends on the amount of power that she can generate from her peers. For example, it could be that she's a magnet to the boys and so becomes socially popular in the eyes of some of the girls who admire that and who hope to get some of the same just by being around her. Or it could be any of the other things I'll explore in this chapter. She'll build up her social identity based on the view of her peers, which will all depend on how worthy and valued they consider her to be: is she worthy of attention and admiration? Is she valued as a 'friend' and protector?

It's the reach of Alpha's social power that's magnetic, and this is what gains her both admirers and her celebrity status.

ALPHA'S STRATEGIES WITH PEERS

Alpha uses four main tools to establish her power: fear, loyalty, popularity and friendship. *Fear* is common to all elements of the system: the alpha female, her pack and her prey. Alpha herself may well be driven by a fear of being alone and powerless, and so to counter this she knows how to create fear in others. She uses fear to create loyalty from others in an incredibly skilful and devious way. She offers them security and safety by accepting them into her pack, from where they will be safe from her own sanctions and punishments. In other words, they won't have to fear being outside the safety of the pack. They'll become 'one of us' and no longer find themselves in the dangerous and precarious position of being one of 'them'. Alpha is well-practised in the art of manipulation. She's an expert at feeding her own needs at the expense of others'. In fact, it's not possible to carry out this type of bullying – creating and sustaining a group of loyal followers – without being incredibly socially skilled and emotionally intelligent. The antisocial alpha female has powerful antisocial resources at her disposal.

Loyalty is something that Alpha has to actively seek out. She needs to be sure that every member of her pack will be loyal to her; that's what will ensure that she stays the leader of the pack. Because she's learned not to trust anything or anyone, she's extra-vigilant about selection procedures and keeping each pack member watchful and fearful. She has to protect herself, be confident that they'll remain loyal and be sure they're committed to keeping her in place against challenges and challengers. She has to be certain they realise that the only way they can stay safe is through becoming dependent on her, by pledging their complete loyalty to her.

To bind the pack to her she offers them a deal. In return for their loyalty she offers them security and something they crave – something that will make them want to feel protective towards her and keep in her in pole position. She offers them *popularity by association*. Popularity isn't difficult for the celebrity alpha. She will have something that others admire. It may be due to sheer luck in the gene pool: she may be prettier and more attractive than those around her. They know it, and so does she. It gets her attention from the boys, and also from the girls who want to be like her and, most importantly, want to be associated with her because her popularity rubs off on them.

On the other hand, her popularity could be due to being tough, or clever, or sporty, or loud, or angry, or breaking rules, or answering teachers back. Each of these qualities will find willing supporters among her peers who find these traits impressive and admirable. She does these things brilliantly, with style, and her potential pack members long to be associated with her. Someone like Danny (aged 15), for example: 'If that person's popular then [others]'ll want to be with them. You see those people in the press that are good at stuff … loved by everyone.' And, of course, once in place, Alpha sets the rules, and then whatever she thinks she *isn't*, she won't want anyone else in the pack to be. So if she isn't pretty she won't like those who are; if she's academically gifted she'll be scornful of those who aren't. They're unlikely to be in her pack; in fact, they may well be on her list of potential prey.

While popularity works like a magnet for Alpha attracting the kind of loyal support she craves, she constantly needs to find new ways to become even more powerful and attractive. So she has one more ace up her sleeve; one more crucially attractive gift that potential pack members can't be confident about getting elsewhere. She offers them the precious hand of friendship.

In reality, of course, it's a completely false friendship that she offers; the kind that has a deceptive veneer of trust, loyalty and reciprocal caring and sharing. It takes in the gullible; those who are deceived by her status, strength and popularity. It is, in fact, a relationship founded on totally conditional terms, lacking any mutual respect, manipulating the notion of 'best friends forever' and the leverage gained from the acquisition of personal secrets as insurance against disloyalty and betrayal.

ALPHA'S STRATEGIES WITH ADULTS

It's not just peers that Alpha skilfully manipulates. She also has brilliant strategies for managing adults. She applies these skills to both teachers and parents. With teachers she's artful at getting herself noticed. She'll work to get them thinking she's clever, or cunning, or misunderstood in an acceptable and forgivable way. If it gets her what she wants she can makes herself liked, and smile her way out of trouble. She knows how to play teachers off against each other, knowing particularly which ones to keep on side. For example, she might work hard to gain good grades because she knows that will please a particular teacher; she knows that teacher also needs her to get good grades. Or she might go out of her way to offer a helping hand when a spare pair of hands is exactly what's needed. She has a hundred and one manipulative strategies to get them to fall under her spell, to be disarmed by her charm offensive, so they join with her rather than rant and rail against her.

In fact, the most skilful and manipulative alphas have the ability to create a spirit of 'friendship' with the teachers they decide to use their charm on. And these teachers fall for it because Alpha is so skilful at offering that feeling of value and worth to anyone who is useful. She can make a member of staff feel great, that she is the only one worth listening to. And once the job is done, Alpha can go out and lead her pack, safe in the knowledge that she has even more protection than before – for now she has the tacit support of figures in authority.

Alpha also knows well how to manipulate parents or carers. Where she feels it necessary, she can acquire even more power and security through the manipulation of parents – whether supportive or indifferent – who may experience a different Alpha at home. Or they simply can't believe what they are told about her school behaviour by concerned teachers, or maybe they just don't want to hear or know. Another factor, of course, is that they might refuse to accept that her behaviour is in any way bullying: 'it's just being assertive,' they say, 'and what's wrong with that?' For these and many other reasons, when parents are summoned to school following an 'incident' it's not at all unusual for them to deny that their daughter is a bully. As one teacher explained to me: '[Her mum] thinks she can do no wrong, [she's] in denial, won't have any of it. [She] thinks, no, not my daughter. Mum won't acknowledge it. She won't say, "Come on, let's sort it out" … That makes [these girls] powerful; [that's how] they can then bully and dominate teachers.'

This kind of obstructive and unhelpful parent behaviour seriously disempowers school staff who are seeking to implement effective anti-bullying policies. And it simply plays into Alpha's hands, giving her yet another route to enhance her power and sense of security

Even with all this tacit, and sometimes even overt, backing from some teachers and parents, Alpha is constantly vigilant. She's very skilful and cunning at not being caught. That's because nothing will ever be her fault. She'll always be able to point the finger at another member of her pack. And she'll have reason, because she doesn't do anything directly herself. She'll have sent one or more of her pack to carry out the bullying work, because that's what you do when you're a pack member. You do what you're told like the loyal lieu-tenant and friend that you are. And you also do it because you're scared of the consequences of Alpha's displeasure, the fear of being thrown out of the pack. Without a word being said, each member of the pack senses what Alpha requires: they watch, they obey, they seek her approval, they avoid whatever will upset her. As thirteen-year-old Georgia explains, 'If they're a leader it's because there are others in the group that are scared. If you get in the group and there's a person that hasn't been bullied, they won't wanna leave that group because they've seen what happens.'

SELECTION OF THE PACK

Security is paramount in Alpha's world view. She's worked hard to get to the top and she wants to stay there. She puts a lot of attention and energy into vetting who she'll include and who she'll exclude from her pack. She'll carry out a very careful selection process. Her emotional intelligence will be working overtime; her selection criteria are focused like the most stringent personality tests. She has to select potential members of her pack with the greatest of care and the unhealthiest of friendship criteria.

One by one she will offer them a chance to join her. She may pretend a veneer of friendship to see how they react. She may elicit secrets, to show them that she is sharing her deepest secrets with them, but she won't be. She's too clever for that; she won't make herself vulnerable. She'll play with friendship skills. She'll give the other girls an elaborate show of how much she cares for them and then wait to see if they return her approaches with signs of genuine trust and loyalty. She'll give potential new recruits initiation tests. For example, she might send them off to carry out some tasks in order to test their willingness and commitment to her – such as delivering 'messages' to potential victims via words, looks or body language, or asking them to retrieve gossip from various quarters. And as they do this, she'll watch like a hawk for the level of their commitment to her orders.

Those who succeed will take the unspoken oath of loyalty and offer her trust in return for friendship and protection. Two fifteen-year-olds, Nicky and Mia, explain why and how this process happens:

> Nicky: I have people who I'm friends with because I know if I'm friends with them no one will touch me. It's like when you hang round with people [who] bully people and no one will say anything to you because [that person's] top dog.

> Mia: If you get [to] be by someone hard, no one will get you 'cause you're hard too.

After the selection process, roles will be allocated within the pack's hierarchy. One of these will be the alpha's second in command. Let's call her Beta. She'll be content to take her orders from Alpha, but she's quite capable of being strong when necessary. Beta will support Alpha through thick and thin. She'll protect her, support her, and carry out Alpha's orders when required. She's the social identity enforcer for Alpha. But Alpha must choose her carefully. If the right circumstances arise, Beta might launch a takeover bid if the pack are behind her.

The rest of the pack forms around Alpha and Beta to become the reinforcers. They all have a desperate need to feel safe and to belong, and a craving to bask in the glow of their association with Alpha. Finally, there will be one, just one, who is the little wolf at the very fringe of the pack. The one that's useful as long as she doesn't do anything wrong; the one that Alpha deliberately keeps there as a potential scapegoat when she needs to instil fear and assert her power. She's called Omega. She's the frail one with a painfully fragile self-concept and even lower self-esteem. Neither Omega nor the pack have any idea just how valuable Omega is to Alpha, but if – and when – the time comes they will get a lesson in power and fear.

As the pack forms, elements emerge that reflect the usual glue of social life. These are at the heart of girl bullying. Central to these elements is the role of friendship. The social glue of friendship, and the loyalty that goes with it, helps the pack become cohesive as they share the common need for friends, a sense of belonging, the need to feel valued and worthy, of being part of a 'family', of being one of us'. These needs are not only the necessary criteria for being a member of the pack; they also reflect Alpha's needs. She needs a pack, she needs a loyal 'family' around her and she has a need to belong. But she also wants something more. She craves *control*. She wants absolute authority over that sense of belonging, over who's in and who's out of her pack. She is Alpha – top dog, head of the pack, leader and protector of her 'school family'.

As in most families, codes of conduct will be established. Unspoken vows of commitment will be made, in particular around serving the needs of Alpha: respect, affiliation and being utterly loyal to the 'family'. In essence, it's the Mafia code: either you're committed to the family or you're an enemy. There is no middle ground as far as Alpha is concerned. It's all or nothing. If a pack member attempts to smuggle a sleeping bag into an outsider's sleepover and stay the night with them, she'll risk Alpha's scorn. Some kind of sanction, punishment or rejection could be due: perhaps being thrown out of the pack or undergoing some kind of social humiliation. The rejection will be framed as a betrayal of the pack. But in reality it's Alpha's feelings of betrayal that will trigger the rejection. Nothing is said but, deep down, every member learns the lesson: be loyal or you're history.

Once Alpha's group is formed they wear their pack badges with pride, happy to be labelled and recognised as members of Alpha's group. After all, what's the point of being in a pack or a gang if you can't draw a big thick dividing line between *us* and *them?* We know who we are because we know who we're not! And as the pack welcomes others labelling them as Alpha's pack, it gives them false justification to label others. The labels the pack gives to others are arbitrary and generally based on personal or group whims: *she looked at me, she's weird, she's fat, she's thin, she's just there.* And if none of those labels and excuses can be applied – well, they'll just find something else that will.

THE VICTIMS

For many years, research into the profiles of victims and bullies has revolved around the ideas of submissive/dominant, passive/aggressive, victim/bullies (Olweus, 1978). I have touched on these issues in previous chapters and have discussed how roles can be interchangeable, depending on circumstance and context. For example, someone who is a bully in the playground may be a victim at home or a bystander in other contexts. When we notice children showing signs of possible 'victim' behaviour at school – for example, social isolation, withdrawing, quality of schoolwork in decline, absence and so on – we should recognise that this is likely to be the result of a combination of factors that have been developing over time. A combination, as we have seen, of dispositional, situational and systemic factors. We need to ask ourselves: what is actually going on?

If a child's previous friendship group has dispersed, or she has no clearly identifiable friends, she'll be a strong candidate for the pack's bullying attentions. Responsible adults are central to noticing these symptoms of vulnerability. The girls who are likely to become targets for Alpha and her pack are like injured gazelles, limping, alone and unable to defend themselves. These are the girls who often don't participate in school activities; the ones who withdraw to the edges of school life. Their self-esteem and self-confidence will have become so low that they'll have neither the energy nor the will to try to outrun the pack or face them. A second common victim type the pack likes to pick on are those who are unaware of social hierarchies and the rules of playground engagement. Maybe they are too quirky, too loud, too isolated, too 'uncool'.

Whatever the rules of engagement, they will have been built to Alpha's own design. They will be arbitrary and therefore difficult to fathom for both children and others who aren't in on the secret. They can be drawn up around what you do and don't wear. What you do and don't watch on TV. How you do and don't behave in a classroom. Who you do and don't look at. And if a rule is breached, Alpha will be ready to pounce, to take down the already vulnerable or socially unaware child.

In my opinion, if Alpha can spot her potential prey then others should be able to do so too. Anti-bullying work is often tuned into bullying behaviour alone and fails to consider how to take action to protect and support the victims *before* they become prey to Alpha and her pack. In other words, while it's important to be watchful for bullying acts in the first place, adults and other responsible citizens, including peers and older students, also need to be on the lookout for potential victims, and be more proactive in their support before Alpha gets her claws into them and before they are bullied. When this is done, strategies can be put in place to help victims to reintegrate, and to rebuild and re-nurture their self-esteem and self-confidence. The alternative is to wait and try to pick up the pieces after the event. But by then, of course, it might be too late. The social and psychological damage will have already been done.

Too often, though, this doesn't happen. So let's consider the consequences of what happens when victims are not noticed or are offered inadequate support. The victim may have had friends, but Alpha will make it clear to them that unless they give up all associations and connections with their former friend, they will become victims too. One by one, Alpha will pick them off. We heard Jodie talk about this in the Introduction: 'She told everyone that I'd told her not to speak to me … She followed me at break times saying nasty comments, turned my friends against me.'

Once a child is socially isolated from other children she becomes easy pickings for Alpha. Alpha will deal with her in one of two ways. She can take the socially vulnerable girl into the 'safety' of her pack. She'll make a 'friend' of her, discover her most precious secrets, so that she'll have potent ammunition to use against her: maybe she'll force her to carry out unpleasant tasks or she'll use the information later to humiliate or blackmail her. Alpha, in her 'generosity', will be seen to offer her victim protection and she'll give her the title of Omega, the weakest and lowliest member of the pack. Alpha's other choice is to pounce immediately. She'll tear her victim to shreds and leave her both psychologically injured and socially disabled. She'll be shunned by everyone because they'll be scared. They won't want to be seen with a victim of Alpha's and they certainly won't want to be next. Starved of the lifeline and support of friendship, the victim will struggle to feel wanted, worthy or valued – certainly at school, maybe in other contexts too. If she has low levels of resilience, a lack of support at home, and a lack of protection and intervention at school, she could easily end up exporting her victim status from school to the wider world. She, like so many other women, many of whom I've worked with, could end up being bullied and feeling devalued and worthless in their work and in their adult relationships.

On the other hand, deliberately applied interventions and strategies to promote self-esteem and self-awareness among those identified as possible or potential victims can become the foundation of a successful process of reintegration and social confidence-building. In my view, early intervention could greatly reduce the long-term impact of girl bullying. The process would also provide a powerful deterrent for the abusers themselves. When I asked alpha females who accepted that they have been or still are bullies the direct question, 'What would have stopped you bullying someone?', the predominant answer was extraordinarily revealing. They say that it is the victim's weakness and helplessness that attracts them. It is not their responsibility but the victim's! As with all wolves, the combined smell of blood and easy prey is compelling. These are typical comments from two fifteen-year-olds:

> Jamie: The person that lacks power needs to stand up for themselves.
>
> Cara: People get more confident and stronger with [being bullied]; they learn to get stronger. People just got to toughen up.

Some of the girls interviewed had been bullied themselves and they believed that it had made them stronger. However, this is rarely the case for victims of girl bullying. For the vast majority, the main effect is the erosion – and even destruction – of their sense of self-esteem and self-worth.

THE BYSTANDERS

We make it very clear that children will be punished [for bullying], and parents say '[but] they weren't doing anything'. And I say, 'Well, they did; they just stood there [doing nothing about it].' (School staff member)

This staff member was talking to me about pupils failing to report bullying. She was explaining the importance of making it clear to pupils that standing by is not a passive act, but an active engagement in the support and toleration of bullying. This is not to say that teachers want students to put themselves at risk by directly intervening when they see bullying going on or about to take place. Rather, she was referring to the strategy that is embedded in many schools that engage in child-centred, practical anti-bullying interventions: 'see it – report it'. Wherever students have bought into this simple but powerful practice, there is a good chance of reducing the likelihood of pupils simply standing by and just watching. It encourages them to take action and report these incidents.

The terms 'bystander apathy' and 'diffusion of responsibility' are frequently used in psychology. The first simply means that bystanders become apathetic, used to what they are seeing. This could be because it has become commonplace due to the normalisation of girl bullying that we explored in Chapter 4. It could also be due to students and adults alike becoming desensitised to the humiliation and abuse of others because of their exposure to the media, as we also saw in Chapter 4. Finally, it could be due to a very real fear of reprisal from the wolf pack.

Diffusion of responsibility is a socio-psychological phenomenon whereby a person is less likely to take responsibility for action or inaction when others are present. How does this work in the context of girl bullying? A common scenario is that Alpha needs an audience that extends beyond her pack. She needs others to see and feel the extent of the power she can exert. However, within that audience will be young people who want to see Alpha's power challenged and who will want to protect potential and actual victims. There will be a natural tendency to think about reporting what they have witnessed. But right next to them are other peers, who they assume are just as responsible for reporting what's going on. So the 'why me?' syndrome comes into play. Why should I be the one to do it, when probably someone else will? Why should I take the risk of reprisal? If I leave it to others I'll avoid the hassle and risk, and I won't need to get involved. And in this way it's all too easy for everyone to become a bystander, complacently pretending to themselves that surely someone else will report what's going on. And so the responsibility for reporting is diffused among the group and no one acts.

The tendency to inaction that comes from these two factors – bystander apathy and diffusion of responsibility – plays into the hands of bullies and the wolf pack and can have serious consequences. Although not a school bullying incident, the following tragic story illustrates what can happen when no one takes responsibility for reporting abusive, aggressive or violent behaviour.

> One summer night in a high profile case, in August 2007, Sophie left her home for an evening out with her boyfriend, Rob. On their way back they walked through a local park where approximately forty other young people were 'hanging out'. Within two minutes of Sophie and Rob arriving, four youths launched an unprovoked attack on Rob. Sophie's mother Sylvia explains what happened next.

> 'It was described as an animalistic, frenzied attack on Rob. Sophie went to help. She knelt over him and cradled his head. Then the youths violently attacked her. After thirteen days on life support, Sophie died. At any one time in the park that night, there had been up to forty young people close by. I understand the fear and horror of the bystanders, but I'm shocked beyond words that no one felt they could help.'

RESPONSIBILITY: WHOSE JOB IS IT ANYWAY?

Alpha knows how easy it is to remain in place, thanks to uncritical social and cultural norms and bystanders' apathy or fears of reprisal. She might not even recognise her actions as unacceptable, because throughout her school years no one in authority has ever seriously challenged them. Unless she's overthrown by a competitive beta, she could well stay top dog until romantic relationships become a stronger magnet for her or the pack than 'best friends forever'; or until she leaves school, or is challenged and dethroned in some way. There is, of course, one other important scenario. She'll find it much harder to stay in place if effective intervention strategies are put in place, reinforced rigorously and shared by the whole school community, including parents, and, if the incident requires legal intervention, the police.

SUMMARY

We have seen how the pack is recruited, mobilised and sustained. Alpha has some very clear needs. She needs to lead, to be acknowledged and to experience a sense of power and control. We can also recognise that she has astute social skills: in a warped, antisocial way she is very emotionally intelligent. These needs and skills can be challenged, addressed and adapted through skilfully applied anti-bullying strategies that allow her to maintain her strong social identity but in a far more pro-social way. But we, and the young people involved in all this, can only begin effective work on these challenges when we bear in mind the lessons of this chapter and the previous ones: in particular, the social contexts that give rise to the potential for bullying; the dispositional, situational and systemic factors; and the specific roles played by alphas, pack members, victims and bystanders, as I have explored in this chapter.

In order to work with girl bullying in this way we'll need to challenge all young people to think in new ways about concepts such as popularity, status, power and friendship. For example, what might be the criteria for the development of really healthy friendships, rather than the manipulative, exploitative ones that tend to exist in the wolf pack? When this process is established and young people begin to find ways of distinguishing for themselves between healthy and unhealthy relationships, empowering and disempowering friendships, the attraction and kudos of belonging to the pack can be more easily understood – and also seen for what it really is.

Most young people have a natural need to belong. It's an essential part of their development: finding ways of being and working together in collaborative groups and dealing with the frictions and conflicts that will inevitably arise. They'll seek out like-minded groups, they may have several friendship groups or just one, maybe they prefer to be more of a leader or more of a follower, and that might shift from group to group. Each one will want to feel she has value, esteem and worth in the eyes of others in their group. Above all, she'll want to feel relatively safe and secure.

Ideally, this is the social context that should be a given in all school playgrounds and other environments where young children come together. Creating this is the task ahead of us. And it's a task not just for those in authority but for those children who are the natural leaders in their groups.

Alpha is a natural leader and she needs to have supporters and admirers around her. But she's been using her leadership skills in a way that – at the end of the day – really serves only herself. Very often she's using these antisocial tactics and strategies to prevent others from seeing the fear and vulnerability she feels herself. She needs help, compassion and understanding as much as she needs to be challenged and confronted. She needs support so that she can discover different skills and strategies to protect herself from her inner fears and vulnerabilities. She needs to be helped so she can find ways of using her leadership skills and her undoubted emotional intelligence to serve the community rather than enslave it.

That is the task to which we have to address ourselves: helping her to turn herself around so that she can become a useful member of the community, instead of a predator.

The sooner victims and potential victims are identified, the better. The longer the time lag, the more damage – social and psychological – is done, which makes it all the harder to help a victim rebuild her confidence, self-esteem and self-worth. Strategies will need to be found and applied to help her overcome any residual sense of isolation and fear of attack. She'll need support to help her reintegrate into one or more friendship groups and discover again a sense of belonging and the ability to trust. It will be important to help her develop her strengths and find ways to address and overcome areas where she feels less confident. Girl bullying is pervasive and reaches into every corner of school life, and so it is important that a support package be implemented beyond the playground in order to effectively change a child's experiences.

Finally, bystanders need to be encouraged and empowered to feel more involved and to take action. A good starting point would be to ensure that everyone recognises that it is their personal responsibility to report any incidents of potential or actual bullying. Then multiple reporting channels need to be put in place that allow observers and witnesses to have easy access. They will also need to be confident that their anonymity is guaranteed to protect them from possible retribution. The aim of all these strategies is to mobilise bystanders by giving them as many opportunities as possible to engage safely and effectively in pro-social action.

If we are to successfully overcome the blight of bullying, we need to promote effective interventions by considering the needs of everyone involved and addressing them in a tailored way. As I discuss in Chapter 6 and in Part 2, this begins by introducing pro-active strategies.

Chapter 6

CYBERBULLYING: THE REALITY OF VIRTUAL AGGRESSION

INTRODUCTION

So far I have considered face-to-face bullying and indirect methods of harassment used by girls. In this chapter I'll explore the use of technology in bullying behaviours. I want to consider what cyberbullying is, how it works, the impact it has and the profiles of people who engage in it.

These days young people have a world of communication and information technology at their fingertips. Opportunities for learning, accessing educational resources and building large social networks have increased beyond anything previous generations could have imagined as teenagers. Having access to technology is second nature to today's children and young people. I didn't even have a computer at the age of fifteen, yet now my three-year-old granddaughter skims screens with her finger and confidently finds whatever cartoon, image or song she's looking for, or accesses the details of the person her mum wants to Skype. She looks at me as though I'm insane when I tell her how clever she is. Someday I'll have to explain to her that, when I was a young girl, phone calls were made in the living room with my parents listening in and a strict time limit was imposed on my conversations. The idea of privacy didn't even come into it.

These days, of course, privacy is a 'norm' in young people's social networking lives. Speed and quantity of information is no longer measured in the number of days it used to take for a letter to arrive and the number of pages it contained, but is almost instantaneous and measured in megabytes and gigabytes. If it's desired, communication with friends can be 24/7 – daytime, night-time, dawn, sunset, mealtimes, leisure time, holidays, sick days, any time you want. And it's delivered through a plethora of channels: texts, photos, Instagrams, comments, emoticons, blogs and comments on social networking sites like Facebook, Twitter and MySpace. And while in my day letters were generally written to special friends, today people communicate with online 'friends' they may never even have met.

This is how young people now interact and connect. Many of them have no idea how they'd live without the internet. Recently, while talking about this with a focus group of fifteen-year-olds, one of them, Becky, looked incredibly pensive and asked the others, 'What would happen if we didn't have social networks?' The response was a stunned silence, eventually interrupted by Anje who said, 'I wouldn't go out, 'cause I'd have no social life,' and Chels, who added, 'I'd just watch TV.'

Just as these young people have no idea how, during my teenage years, I organised my time to play with school friends, I have no real idea how they manage their social networking lives. I know it's a life that involves multiple conversations on the go at once, where news travels fast and lots of little pixels form immediate images that can be sent in seconds to tens, hundreds and even thousands of young people almost anywhere on the planet.

But, of course, the internet and all the associated media that goes with it is a double-edged sword. It makes many wonderful things possible, but it's also open to abuse. The downside of multiple messaging, instantaneous communication and the distribution of personal photographs and information is that it can so easily lead to a huge magnification of harassment, humiliation and personal denigration. The mass distribution of bullying messages is always only a fingertip away from internet users who choose to abuse its potential. And what makes it so much more cynical – and clinical – is that the cyberspace distance between the sender and the receiver of those messages or images means that the sender never sees the reaction and may not be aware of the hurt and humiliation she causes.

One of the conclusions reached by Professor Tanya Byron in her 2008 report for the DfE, *Safer Children in a Digital World*, was that the distance offered by technological communication often leads to impulsive behaviours that might not otherwise happen in face-to-face interactions. It seems the distance between sender and recipient can play an important role in understanding why cyberbullying is so pervasive and so challenging to tackle.

The impact of cyberbullying is not always immediate. Not all children have their phones or other devices switched on all day. In fact, they may not even know they've been subjected to cyber-abuse until they walk into school the next day or until they power up their phone or tablet to check their social networking sites. The humiliation of not knowing that they were a victim of cyberbullying, the thought that people were laughing at them behind their back, the shame of not being up to speed with events, can be devastating.

They feel they are the last ones to know what's actually happening in their own life.

Cyberbullying is relentless and pervasive, which can make the suffering it brings feel non-stop. Its 24/7 nature leaves victims with nowhere to hide. The huge 'audiences' involved in social networking communications lead receivers of bullying, intimidating or abusive messages to experience a profound sense of powerlessness. They feel there's nothing they can do to stem the overwhelming tide of humiliation in the face of such numbers. The social network a person belongs to can be destroyed with one message. Vicious rumours can be spread at the touch of a button. And messages can be anonymous, or have multiple senders, or a limitless number of supporters who 'like' the message, or bystanders who don't actively support the thread but don't challenge it either.

All this links very closely to some of the issues I've already discussed with regard to school playgrounds and elsewhere, in the sense that the lack of a clear definition of bullying, or the absence of healthy models of social behaviour, mean that many children often don't realise they are doing anything wrong. And in cyberbullying it's the very lack of face-to-face interaction, the sense of virtual distance, that can prevent those involved from connecting their actions with bullying behaviour. Distanced by cyberspace from the recipient, they see the comments, emoticons, messages and images they send as innocuous – when in truth they can often be more socially and psychologically destructive than incidents that occur in the playground. Receiving a bullying message on your personal phone or tablet can be a very lonely and heartbreaking experience.

So in the rest of this chapter I want to look more deeply at what cyberbullying is and how it happens, how it relates to girl bullying in general, what happens when girls and others treat cyberbullying as a separate type of bullying and the role played by bystanders. I'll also consider why reporting incidents of internet and phone bullying is even more problematic than reporting face-to-face incidents, particularly given the fact that devices such as tablets and mobile phones are such an integral part of a young person's private life.

HOW MUCH OF A PROBLEM IS CYBERBULLYING?

Cyberbullying is huge. It's on the increase and is invading the lives of more and more young people every year. It's both obvious and subtle, just like playground bullying but worse. It's pervasive and brutal; sometimes the perpetrators are unseen and anonymous. It's a very public 'dissing' that is witnessed by a potential audience of thousands.

In previous chapters I have discussed how traditional girl bullying impacts on victims. But there's always a glimmer of hope with playground bullying, because the bully is physically limited to her 'patch' and to school hours. Sanctuary is usually available in locations where the bully and her wolf pack are not present, where they're off-limits or choose not to go. Cyberbullying, however, offers no such sanctuary, yet brings with it all the traditional abuses of girl bullying. The reason is plain to see. There is no escape from the presence of computers, mobile phones and tablets in most homes these days, and who wants to be seen at the leisure club, sports club or play park without the status and comfort of their device? The mobile phone or tablet, 'cool' symbol and storage unit of one's personal and social standing, has become for many the ever-present dumping ground for the spite and malice of the bully. These days, being at home can feel as threatening as being at school. More and more young people in the UK are being drawn into this nightmare every day.

In the UK, research appears to agree that about 40% of young people have been actively exposed to cyberbullying. Of these, only 22% have spoken to someone about it. According to one UK charity (ChildLine, 2014), in 2014 there was an 87% increase in children who had been cyberbullied compared to in 2011. Another report (Ditch the Label, 2014) indicated that bullying via social networking sites, as reported by young people, was shown to be the highest on MySpace (89%) and on Facebook (54%). The report noted catastrophic effects on self-esteem and social lives in up to 70% of the young people affected. In the USA, Burgess-Proctor et al. (2010) reported the online behaviour and experiences of over 3,000 girls aged eight to seventeen. They found that over 80% of the respondents had been bullied online and 20% didn't know who had bullied them. The two most common online bullying behaviours reported were being ignored (left out of conversations) (46%) and being disrespected (43%). The girls also stated that cyberbullying made them feel 'sad', 'angry', 'depressed', 'violated', 'helpless', exploited, 'stupid and put down'. Others reported having suicidal thoughts. So, what exactly is cyberbullying and how does it evolve?

WHAT IS CYBERBULLYING?

In Chapter 1, I discussed the difficulties that arise in generating an acceptable and all-embracing definition of girl bullying. Similar challenges often present themselves in defining cyberbullying, but this is mainly because it's usually seen as a *type* of bullying, whereas in my view it's actually more of an extended *method* for bullying. In this case, a definition can be shared with traditional girl bullying simply by expanding the description.

At the end of Chapter 1 I offered the following definition of bullying:

> Bullying consists of a complex web of antisocial behaviours that not only includes physical intimidation but also verbal harassment, belittling verbal and non-verbal signals, the abuse of power, aggressive actions, the aggressive manipulation of friendships and the deliberate intention to cause a victim to feel distressed, humiliated or socially isolated.

With this definition in mind, let's take a look at some of the methods used in internet and phone bullying and see what's similar and what's different.

Based on research and findings by Smith et al. (2013), Cross et al. (2009) and Hinduja and Patchin (2008), methods of cyberbullying include:

● Exclusion or antisocial treatment through online games.

● Flaming: causing online verbal fights.

● Cyber-stalking.

- Sending threatening messages.

- Sending insulting or denigrating messages, or put-downs that cause distress or anxiety.

- Creating, sending or sharing offensive images.

- Sending sexual messages, or sending messages that pressure someone into sexual acts or into taking sexually explicit images of themselves or others and then forwarding them.

- Posting distressing, humiliating, embarrassing or threatening messages or texts on social media sites.

- Stealing an online identity to cause distress or anxiety.

- Creating hate sites or burn books (online books that contain bitchy comments about others, including friends).

- Sending inappropriate messages in real time on chatlines, games, blogs or conversations that cause distress or anxiety.

- Making silent or hoax calls.

- Exclusion (from an online group).

- Masquerading (pretending to be someone else when posting material in order to damage the perceived sender).

- Any form of online harassment, humiliation, defamation of character, denigration or rumour-mongering.

It's not difficult to see the many similarities between cyberbullying and face-to-face girl bullying, including exclusion, intimidation, abusive messages, threats, dissing and defamation of character. Yet there also appear to be some differences, such as hoax and silent calls, blogs and the posting of messages. But are these actually differences in *type*, or are they really just differences in *method*? When we stop to think about it, blogs are really no different from gossip; posting malicious messages is no different from spreading rumours; and hoax and silent calls are not very different from Alpha sending out her pack to deliver threatening messages or inviting someone to a party that doesn't exist. In my view, cyberbullying strategies are very similar indeed to the more traditional methods of girl bullying. It seems to me that established techniques have just been migrated into more contemporary forms. The devices – the tablets and phones – have simply displaced to some extent the role of the wolf pack.

If I'm right, we still have to consider the differences that this use of technology makes to the bully, the victims, the bystanders and the 'interveners': the adults, parents, and responsible peers. Smith et al. (2013) describe seven features to help us distinguish between the uses of technology in bullying and traditional bullying:

- A degree of technological expertise is required.

- It is indirect and potentially anonymous.

- The perpetrator is distanced from seeing the victim's reaction.

- The roles of the bystanders are more complex.

- The motives are less clear: in particular, the status of the bully may not always be increased when cyberbullying.

- The size of audience is much greater.

● There is no safe haven for victims.

As research moves closer to agreeing a definition for cyberbullying, the girls themselves appear to be doing everything they can to explain away their online behaviour as perfectly normal. In my focus groups, I had extensive discussions with girls aged from thirteen to fifteen about what cyberbullying behaviour is and how it works. But every time I challenged them about questionable behaviour, they continually responded that 'sticking up for friends can't be called bullying' or 'we're just making comments'. It seemed that the lack of face-to-face connection appeared to allow these girls to dilute cyberbullying behaviour into something perfectly normal and innocuous. Here's thirteen-year-old Kirsty:

> If there's an argument on Facebook I have to get myself involved 'cause I'm bored and have to make a comment. I just comment with a laughing face and get called a bully. But [I'm] not, it's just a laughing face. I just like to read through the comments.

And thirteen-year-old Mitchelle said:

> I just put a comment on and then they said I had bullying issues.

It seems there's a dividing line between what adults see as cyberbullying and how young people view their online behaviour. As I've already noted, this is also the case with traditional bullying, except in this context the roles are reversed. In the context of cyberbullying it's the young people who are normalising the bullying behaviour and saying 'it's just girls being girls'.

HOW IT WORKS

These days girls use whatever technology is available to develop and manage their social relationships and friendships. And so do girl bullies. Some of the girls in one of my focus groups had an impromptu discussion between themselves about who had the most friends on Facebook. Thirteen-year-old Kirsty said, 'A lot goes off on Facebook, like how many "likes" [you have]', to which thirteen-year-old Anna added, 'Facebook is … really important if someone's got 300-odd friends.' There was little evidence from what they said that those 'friends' were relationships based on mutual support or respect. But getting a large number of 'likes' did seem to provide an element of status: of being wanted, of being popular and of being associated with a popular peer. Sadly, the reverse is also true. Technology also makes available negative markers of social acceptance: you can be unwanted, unpopular and 'un-liked'. Quite brutally, you can be 'unfriended'.

It seems to me that the very natural urge to belong, the need to have friends, no matter who they are, and the desire to be included in the group can swell the numbers of bystanders in cyberbullying in the same way as in the playground. The fear that one might be thrown out of the pack, or picked on or intimidated, if one doesn't join in, or if one reports what is going on, could still be at play. This could explain why so many young people who would otherwise be bystanders feel the need to add their contribution to abusive or dissing messages even if they are 'just making comments'. They see this as behaviour that keeps them in the pack, or in Alpha's good books, depending on their role. At the very least, it's what keeps them from appearing on Alpha's radar as a potential victim themselves. It also gives Alpha more social power if it seems that she has many followers. With a high number of 'friends' appearing to support her, how can she fail to impress, or strike fear among, those who fall within reach of her social networks, whether online or offline?

In the study mentioned earlier in the chapter, Smith et al. (2013) point out that cyberbullying doesn't always allow for social status to be gained through bullying actions. But when it does the impact is huge, and the support and 'friending' she gets massively increases Alpha's social networking status. For example, when Alpha posts comments, status updates or images on Facebook she reaches all her 'friends'. If those 'friends' comment, the images are then forwarded to their 'friends'. And so the number of bystanders multiplies inexorably. Similarly, although without the same multiplication velocity, sending a text message to 'all contacts' increases the impact of the message at the press of a button. Cyberbullying is overwhelming and powerful because of its ability to humiliate victims through the vast numbers who are potentially involved, and because it happens in the blink of an eye and at the press of a key.

Cyberbullying means Alpha can save energy on face-to-face abuse and intimidation. It allows her to humiliate from a distance, signing off her message as either a known or unknown sender. But most alphas are extroverts. She needs an audience, and sitting alone in a room sending anonymous messages really doesn't serve her status at all well. So she uses cyber methods in ways that enhance her social standing and status. For example, she might gather her pack in the corner of the playground, and rather than sending out a messenger to deliver the 'look' or a jibe, she will simply send an electronic message as the pack watches. In this case it's a mixture of cyber- and playground bullying, but it's far less effort for far more impact.

Another strategy might see Alpha having a sleepover with her pack. Part of the entertainment might be finding time to write and send a victim abusive messages, or to run a group discussion on which picture to select and distribute that will most humiliate a victim, or ex-pack member. The group might also create an extra level of evening entertainment by using a cyberbullying 'game'. Alpha needs adoration and so anonymity will be far from her mind, *unless* she fears she might be close to being caught and accused. In that case she will simply use the tactics that have always served her to avoid guilt. She'll get one of the pack, maybe Omega, to use their phone or computer to send the abusive message or image.

The messages and images that Alpha or her minions send will then reach many people. And by the very nature of social networking formats, these will mostly be in the position of bystanders. Theoretically they could all report this information as bullying. But how many will? The depressing answer is very few, if any. It seems that bystander apathy is even more obvious with cyberbullying than it is in traditional bullying. The reason is not hard to fathom. It's just the way social media works. You can forward the message and become a supporter. You can comment on the message and become a supporter. You can put a smiley face emoticon on the message and become a supporter. You can even ignore the message and still become a supporter. Very often, whatever active or passive response is made ends up supporting or reinforcing the bullying message. To those involved, it doesn't seem like bullying; just passing on messages. In this way everybody feels like a bystander and the vast majority are apathetic when it comes to reporting bullying.

Bystander apathy also seems to be closely linked with the sense of distance that exists in young people's minds among all those involved in cyberbullying: senders, bystanders and victims alike. Many young people seem to have a problem recognising any link between dissing someone online, even if it's just adding a 'smiley' to 'approve' a negative message, and the damage and hurt it can cause the receiver. Explaining to young people that a screen doesn't separate them from the impact and effect of their actions on others, whether as bullies or bystanders, is a message many find hard to comprehend. Anje exemplifies how this distancing factor works: 'They hide behind a computer. They think when you're online you're not going to get told off [for bullying]. They think, I'm just typing, it's not real life.' However, it is real life for the victim. Removing the face-to-face element of bullying doesn't reduce its impact. In many cases, the opposite is true.

For the victims, the crowd of supporters only adds to the sadness, anger, depression, violation, helplessness and suicidal thoughts they suffer, as Burgess-Proctor et al. (2010) highlights. Victims can receive abusive messages at any time of the day or night, with no control over their content. The outcome can be not only total isolation from online social networks but also from social networks at school. For a victim who lacks self-esteem in the hurly-burly of the playground, online social networking can be vitally important. They see it as a golden opportunity to communicate with peers and others without awkwardness, without having to worry about all the paraphernalia of social skills that face-to-face communication requires.

Online chat is easier for them. They feel they have some control over interactions. They feel safe in those discussions. And then, just when they think they are getting somewhere, they are sent reeling by online bullying. From a feeling of safety, they are pitched into a nightmare of insecurity, humiliation and denigration. They could report this bullying if they wanted to. But will they? For many it's the only world they feel is theirs; that belongs to them. It's their private world and now it's under threat. How can anyone else help with that? And do they really want to let anyone else read the abusive content with which they've been humiliated?

THE 'PRIVATE' AGENT

Unlike my generation, young people today expect privacy in their communication. They consider it a right to have a private life and private communications. And while that is understandable, it also creates the perfect conditions for cyberbullying because those whose job it is to safeguard young people – parents, carers and teachers – often have no idea at all about what is really going on. Privacy is great in principle, but also a dangerous reality in these circumstances. Few people in this context, whether children or adults, seem to have got their head around the idea that with rights come responsibilities. Some young people are not taking enough responsibility for the damage they are causing through the thoughtless sending or supporting of hurtful messages, and parents often have no idea what kind of messages their children are sending or receiving. And parents often don't ask their children what's going on online because it seems intrusive. The pain and fear felt by many children is hidden behind a conspiracy of silence, held in place by the tyranny of privacy.

This is a huge problem when it comes to managing bullying. How do we help young people to understand that cyberbullying needs to be reported and brought into the open? Unless reporting begins to happen more often, and more willingly, adults will have no way into young people's private communications networks and therefore no way to begin to address cyberbullying. While the obsession for privacy without responsibility remains, Alpha will continue to feel that she can carry on doing exactly as she likes.

CYBERBULLIES: REVERSE PSYCHOLOGY

In this chapter I've talked about bullying migrating to technology, but some alpha bullies neither rate nor use technology to bully. They see it as cowardly. A group of thirteen- to fifteen-year-old girls, who have been alpha female bullies, told me what they thought of cyberbullying and people who carry it out.

> Becky: More scared people [cyberbully].
>
> Mia: [They do it to] make themselves seem big.
>
> Libby: I think [it's] people that are scared to say something to someone face to face.

Nicko: [They] say it behind your face so you can't hit them or anything, then when you go up to them at school and say, 'What the hell do you think you're doing?' they're, like, [scared].

Each one of these girl bullies thought cyberbullies were cowards.

There's one more twist to the profiles of cyberbullies. In another reversal of the playground situation, it is quite possible in the cyberspace arena for Alpha's victim to become her bully; something that would be unthinkable in the playground unless it were to take place over quite a long period of time as the victim toughens herself up in some way and gathers some allies. How is this possible? It's the screen that lends her confidence and protection. It gives her distance, privacy from an audience and anonymity. She feels safer to turn the tables, particularly if she has some additional technological skills. It's her chance to feel some power at last and to gain some retribution.

However, if she thinks this will give her sweet revenge without risk she could be very much mistaken. As we'll discover in the next chapter, anyone engaged in cyberbullying, with the intent to cause harm or distress to others, whether they are bullies, bystanders or those who are victims in other contexts, could find themselves facing serious legal consequences. Many young people are completely unaware of the technological and other resources that are available to law enforcement authorities to unearth the trail of evidence that cyberbullying leaves. Once the authorities are aware that bullying is taking place, its sources can be traced and the perpetrators identified and taken to task.

OPPORTUNITIES FOR INTERVENTION

In cyberbullying we face a growing problem that needs a two-pronged approach: first, reactive strategies such as reprimands and sanctions to keep things in check; second, and much more important, proactive strategies that support young people to turn the issue around for themselves. Education holds the key to all of this.

Opportunities for intervention are often dismissed by teachers and others because the reach of cyberspace extends far beyond the school gates. 'What can we do?' is far too common an attitude. But as I have argued the roles and methods of traditional girl bullying also lie at the heart of cyberbullying. Whatever role a young person is playing in the cyber-arena – bully, reinforcer, bystander or victim – the same basic approaches to proactive change that apply in traditional girl bullying also apply. In this way we will avoid the mistake of treating cyberbullying as a separate, misunderstood and out-of-reach issue.

Another key opportunity for intervention is tackling the thorny issue of privacy. As we have seen, this is a serious obstacle in getting to the root of what is actually going on in cyberbullying. Victims, bullies, bystanders and parents all need to understand the consequences of privacy, its pros and cons, and the importance of taking personal and social responsibility for one's actions, if privacy is not to be abused. Education can help young people, parents and carers to recognise that there are times when privacy is perfectly fine and other times when it puts other people's safety and well-being at risk. The misuse of privacy, particularly when privacy is seen as an unquestionable and inalienable right, without the responsibilities that go with it, is dangerous without safeguards and a clear understanding of the difference between pro-social and antisocial online behaviour. Information technology departments in schools and organisations can play a very important role here in working openly with children and young people to design 'acceptable use' polices for IT, including the responsible use of tablets, mobile phones and social media forums.

Some anti-bullying approaches have suggested the solution to cyberbullying is simply to tell a victim not to use their devices. It's a solution that may seem tempting, even logical, but it fails to tackle the main issues, and it also fails to recognise the central role these devices play in the lives of young people. In fact, cutting them off from their connection with the social world in this way may adversely affect victims, leaving them with even deeper feelings of isolation and separation from peers.

Overall, we need to educate children and young people about the consequences of bullying via technology. This should begin with an understanding that bullying behaviour doesn't always have to be face to face and that online, screen-based bullying has the same intent and outcome as traditional bullying. Both methods have the intention of humiliating or causing harm or distress to the victim. When that intention is evident, the consequences can be serious indeed, both for the victim and for the bully. Young people need to be encouraged, supported and offered guided discussions and other open forums to consider the evidence, showing them the impact and damage that cyberbullying causes. Among other things, this will mean challenging the idea that virtual 'distance' absolves them from blame for bullying or bystanding and that it's not 'just typing'. In fact, it's very real.

Only when we've got beyond the issues of distance and privacy, when we've arrived at the point where young people begin to understand what is and isn't acceptable, and when they've begun to feel able and safe to report abuse and misuse of technological bullying, can reactive measures effectively be applied. Cyberbullying leaves a trail of evidence. Once a thread is identified it can be easily traced and proved. Sanctions include prosecution for the misuse of technology in seeking to deliberately harm the well-being of others. The relevent legislation will be described in Chapter 7.

The fact is that if we don't educate children and young people in the misuse of technology, and if they don't begin to take greater personal and collective responsibility for the way social messages are shared and distributed, not only will more lives be damaged but we will also miss a great opportunity to intervene and reduce incidents of cyberbullying. And if nothing changes, those caught in the net, whether bullies, reinforcers or bystanders, could end up being prosecuted for their cyberbullying behaviour, no matter who they are or why they did it.

SUMMARY

Major problems are looming as cyberbullying becomes more common. Huge numbers of bystanders and reinforcers are involved; far more than are implicated in playground bullying. What makes the situation even worse is the huge gap that exists between what many young people view as perfectly acceptable online behaviour such as 'standing up for my friends' and the actual damage caused to victims of cyberbullying in the real world. Many see cyberspace as a safe place to operate in, a virtual space where their activities are private and more or less harmless. Many think their participation can be all too easily absolved or will even go undetected through the sense of anonymity they get from sending or supporting messages online, or by simply hitting the delete button. Thinking that the internet is a way to bully that is relatively safe from sanctions and consequences is wrong.

Adults have a huge responsibility to help and educate young people to realise that there is no difference between cyberbullying and its more traditional forms. The message has to be clear: there are no excuses for bullying. Perceptions of distance have to be dispelled and the notion of privacy has to be tempered with a sense of responsibility. The myth surrounding the lack of accountability that some young people think cyberbullying offers has to be challenged and laid to rest.

Part of the problem has been caused in recent years by the tendency to categorise cyberbullying as a type of bullying, and in my view this has only served to reinforce an unhelpful separation between online and more traditional forms of bullying. As I've argued in this chapter, it seems to make much more sense to think of cyberbullying as an extension of the traditional methods of bullying, projected into cyberspace. When looked at in this way, we can see that similar definitions apply and similar strategies can be brought to bear. Seeing cyberbullying as an extension of face-to-face harassment and abuse will help. I will explore these strategies, and ways to deal practically with other issues raised in this chapter, in Part 2.

Chapter 7
BULLYING AND THE LAW

INTRODUCTION

Let's now turn our attention to the law and its relationship to bullying issues and behaviours. No one wants to prosecute children, but it's important to understand that bullying – which may include assault, threatening behaviour, harassment and the intention to cause harm and distress – are serious issues that may justifiably attract the attention of the police. If bullying behaviours are considered to be serious enough, then bullies should – and will be – prosecuted. Of course, an early criminal record earned through bullying could blight a young person's future, so it's not something that should be done lightly. We should also remember that it's not only bullying behaviour carried out by individuals that can have legal repercussions: the schools, the teachers and school staff are also at risk of civil or criminal prosecution if they fail to protect children and young people from harm or if they do not adhere to legal guidance when devising and implementing anti-bullying strategies.

In this chapter I want to explore the factors mentioned above as well as the relevant legislation and guidelines that apply to both individual bullying and to failures in the system. I'll also consider how these laws can be used as a starting point for developing educational strategies that can be used to intervene when bullying is suspected or to prevent it from happening in the first place.

The law makes it clear that school staff have a duty of care to protect pupils from harm. The Children Act 1989 states that it is the responsibility of everyone who comes into contact with children, defined as young people under eighteen years of age, to promote strategies that protect them from harm and abuse. Following several high-profile serious case reviews, the Children Act was amended in 2004 to make it clear that safeguarding included the prevention of harm and the promotion of well-being for all children, not only those perceived to be at risk of harm. The Act states that it's the responsibility of everyone who comes into contact with children and young people to implement strategies that protect them from all types of harm and abuse. It also stresses that schools have a duty to protect children from bullying, harassment and discrimination. Sometimes it seems that society in general does not apply the same rules when considering the treatment of young people. Harassment, threats and other intimidating types of behaviour all put other people at risk, whether they are children or adults. When adults are treated in this way, everybody would expect the law to intervene. Surely it's just as important that children and young people are similarly protected? Children, after all, have just as much of a right to lead safe, happy and secure lives as anyone else.

The UK government provides clear legislation on the subject of safeguarding children in all environments. The DfE issued statutory guidance in 2015 called *Keeping Children Safe in Education*. It reads:

> Safeguarding and promoting the welfare of children is defined for the purposes of this guidance as: protecting children from maltreatment; preventing impairment of children's health or development; ensuring that children grow up in circumstances

consistent with the provision of safe and effective care; and taking action to enable all children to have the best outcomes.

(DfE, 2015, p. 5)

The guidance makes the point that if a child isn't adequately safeguarded, then the adults whose role it is to provide such protection must act to improve the situation. If they fail to do so, they may be committing an offence and therefore liable to prosecution.

The laws and guidance make it clear that young people and adults alike need to be aware of the legal implications and consequences of both bullying and for failing to act effectively and consistently to protect children from bullying. In the UK the age of criminal responsibility is ten. This means that it's really important that quality anti-bullying strategies and policies are implemented right from the start of primary schooling.

WHEN BULLYING BEHAVIOUR BECOMES A LEGAL MATTER

It's a legal requirement for state schools in the UK to have a behaviour policy that includes *clear measures to prevent bullying*. The government recommends that this policy is extended to include an anti-bullying policy as well. Most state schools comply with this guidance. Private schools are regulated by their own governing bodies, and many of them also have guidance in place for the provision of anti-bullying polices. Other Acts are also relevant to bullying behaviours. For example, the Equality Act 2010 requires schools and organisations to act in cases of discrimination, harassment or victimisation.

When an incident occurs in school, or out of school between pupils who attend the same school, the behaviour policy and the anti-bullying policy will become central to any potential legal action. Consideration will be given to the content of, and adherence to, the school's policies and safeguarding procedures. It's with this in mind that I have spent many years involved with the development and evaluation of anti-bullying policies. These policies are not simply a box-ticking exercise. They're a clear acknowledgement of the legal requirements, the civil requirements and the *in loco parentis* obligations of the school and its staff. The policies are all about clarifying what is expected and prioritising the welfare and safeguarding of pupils.

The policies are vital for two reasons. First, they provide legal clarification of what constitutes bullying or other antisocial behaviour; and, second, they offer effective proactive and reactive anti-bullying strategies. School staff will need to show that these strategies have been actively applied. Further, these policies and the broad strategies will need to be understood and known to all stakeholders, including staff, parents and pupils. I explore anti-bullying strategies in more detail in Chapter 8.

While many cases of bullying are managed effectively by school staff, especially when clear guidelines and policies are in place, there may be times when a case escalates and requires legal action. In these cases evidence will need to be gathered of aggressive behaviour and the intent to harm, harass or humiliate. These incidents may include physical or verbal abuse, threats and intimidation, abusive text or phone messages, hate messages and racist or homophobic behaviour. Consideration must also be given to the impact of these behaviours on the victim, such as fear, distress and anxiety.

Cases that warrant legal intervention can be dealt with in different ways depending on the severity and frequency of the incidents. At the lower end of the scale, the bully could be given an indirect warning – for example, through a police presentation to a whole-school assembly setting out details of what happens to people who are caught and prosecuted for bullying. Other early stage strategies might be a face-to-face discussion between the perpetrator and a police officer or a moderated face-to-face discussion between the bully and the victim.

A more serious incident could lead directly to legal action being taken. If that happens, an investigation will begin in order to determine whether the pupil(s) have been systematically persecuting or victimising another child through direct or indirect methods. During the investigation consideration will be given to situational factors – for example, the police will talk to school staff, parents and peers. Systemic, situational and dispositional factors will also be considered, such as the perpetrator's behavioural patterns over time and in different places, and the success or otherwise of previous interventional strategies during earlier stages of the escalating situation. If the bullying behaviour is found to be evidenced, persistent and serious enough, a case may be prepared for the Crown Prosecution Service (CPS).

Cases referred to the CPS are considered for prosecution. Some may be brought to trial and could end with a guilty verdict being delivered. If the offender is found guilty, she will have a criminal record. In these cases it is likely that the school or organisation will also be investigated on the grounds of ineffective application of the legislation. If sufficient evidence of failure to safeguard a child or to implement intervention strategies is found, both legal action and disciplinary measures can be taken against the school and or individuals involved. While prosecutions are rare, they do happen. The fallout can be enormous for everyone involved – for the bully and for those who failed to fulfil their responsibility to safeguard children adequately and to prevent bullying behaviours.

ACTS THAT DEAL WITH BULLYING

In the UK there are many Acts of Parliament that are applicable and relevant in cases of bullying. Here is a brief outline of the relevant legislation, both criminal and civil.

Criminal laws

- *Equality Act 2010* – This Act covers discrimination on the grounds of race, gender, disability, age, sexual orientation, religion or belief, and gender reassignment.

- *Communications Act 2003* – This Act covers all forms and types of public communication. With regard to bullying, it covers the sending of grossly offensive, obscene, menacing or indecent communications, and any communication that causes needless anxiety or contains false accusation.

- *Protection from Harassment Act 1997* – This Act covers any form of harassment that has occurred 'repeatedly'; in this instance, 'repeatedly' means on one or more occasions.

- *Computer Misuse Act 1990* – This Act includes hacking into accounts.

- *Malicious Communications Act 1988* – This Act covers the sending of grossly offensive or threatening letters, electronic communications or any other form of message with the intention of causing harm, distress or anxiety.

- *Public Order Act 1986* – This Act covers the intention to cause harassment, alarm and distress; the use of threatening, abusive or insulting words or behaviours; and the writing of signs or forms of visual representation that are likely to cause harassment, alarm or distress.

- *Protection of Children Act 1978* – This Act covers sexual offences and is applicable to all children. The Act states that it is a crime to take, make, permit to take, distribute, show, possess or possess with intent to distribute indecent images of children.

- *Obscene Publications Act 1959 and 1964* – This Act covers the circulation, playing or projecting of articles or data that have the intention to deprave or corrupt those who see or read them (this includes the school intranet).

While criminal law has an important role to play in child-on-child bullying incidents, the UK also has two relevant civil laws.

Civil law

- *Defamation Act 2013* – This Act is relevant when a statement has caused, or is likely to cause, serious harm to the reputation of a person.

- *Crime and Disorder Act 1998* – This Act includes a tiered approach to tackling antisocial behaviour. This allows for proportionate responses to be made, with the intention to protect children from further abuse or to prevent antisocial behaviour escalating into criminal behaviour.

The Acts mentioned above cover all the elements of girl bullying that I have described in previous chapters. The laws are comprehensive, covering all eventualities that may arise. The legislation clearly states that if intent to harm is proven, criminal proceedings will be considered.

One of the most useful and revealing aspects of these laws is that they make it clear that *evidence* of bullying and other antisocial behaviours isn't limited to hard facts alone; behavioural patterns and the history of situational and systemic factors can also be considered. These patterns of behaviour include face-to-face interactions, witness statements, teacher reports and impact on the victim. In the case of cyberbullying, admissible evidence may also include online patterns of communications and the use of IT to harass, intimidate and bully.

'PRIVACY' AND THE LAW

Chapter 6 discussed some of the perceptions that surround the notion of 'privacy'. Two of the central misconceptions held by some children and young people is the idea that bullying via technology is a *private* issue and that evidence can't be accessed or uncovered. In this they are completely wrong.

I have argued that, in my view, cyberbullying is a *method* of threatening, intimidating, harassing and aiming to cause distress to others, and that it needs to be addressed in just the same way as more traditional forms of bullying. So let's consider how the law supports this view and how it can act in relevant cases. I want to shatter any ideas that privacy exists in cyberbullying, that pressing the delete key after sending a malicious message offers any protection or safety, or that the real world is somehow removed from cyber-actions – because, in fact, the real world *is* watching, retrieving the relevant information and is willing to prosecute cyberbullies.

One way to get young people to wake up and take notice is to introduce them to the idea of cyber 'visibility' through a term many of them recognise and acknowledge: their 'digital footprint'. Using technology leaves a *footprint* that can be investigated. It's like a DNA code that can be used to track and identify a perpetrator. Information is also stored on the senders' and receivers' hard disks and on remote servers. So, those Facebook messages that bullies and bystanders think they are 'just typing' in cyberspace can be tracked and used as evidence in a court of law. And it's not just evidence for the police to use if there's an investigation. It's also evidence for parents and teachers to print off. In fact, school staff are

now spending considerable time and energy dealing with issues of cyberbullying among girls.

In this context it's essential that schools have in place clear and authoritative behaviour and anti-bullying policies. The Education and Inspections Act 2006 states that 'to such extent as is reasonable, head teachers have the power to regulate the conduct of pupils when they are off-site or not under the control or charge of a member of staff.' This Act gives school staff who suspect pupils of cyberbullying the legal power to search and confiscate their mobile phones. If they believe that incidents have taken place that contravene the school behaviour/anti-bullying policy, they can request that a pupil reveals a message or shows the content of their phone.

I carried out an extensive interview with Mrs Thomas, who works closely with girls in school as part of her role as a behaviour manager. She talked in detail to me about some of the girl bullying issues that she has to deal with on a daily basis. Here are some excerpts:

> A lot of bullying is online. Facebook. They all join in. We print stuff off and there's reams and reams and names and names, loads of them that have all joined in. If you give the girls the printed [version of their] conversation on Facebook, faces change; they can't deny it. [And] unless you give them hard evidence, parents can't accept their child is doing that. And we get a lot of this if one of the girls sends a boy a[n] [indecent] picture [of herself] that then goes round the school. We've told them: if you take a picture of yourself, it's child porn – you're sending pornography. We have so many lessons about sexting and they still haven't got the message. Week in and week out, I've got girls coming to me in tears because they've sent photos and they've gone around school. They've been told numerous times. Still it doesn't seem to go in. And bullying via

pictures on Facebook: sometimes they've had a fall-out and they say, 'I'll send that photo of you in your bra and knickers jumping on the bed', or that one of you drinking, or smoking a joint. They've got more power [over each other] now because they've got more physical information on each other to put out there if there's a fall[ing]-out.

Mrs Thomas's story is revealing for many reasons. She feels strongly that the school is working tirelessly to educate pupils about the dangers of cyberbullying, but then makes it clear that, for some of the students, the education strategies being implemented are far from effective. I can't help but wonder if this is related to two factors that we discussed earlier in the book: (1) the girls' capacity to separate their cyber-behaviour from real-world behaviour, and (2) their ability to distance themselves from blame or responsibility, partly because of their belief that they won't be caught, and partly because of their view that cyberspace is a private world that no one can invade. There may be another important factor too. The approach to cyber-safety that Mrs Thomas describes is a strategy of 'telling' rather than 'showing' or, even better, 'discovering'. It may well be that a very different approach through discovery learning might be worth exploring and would work better with these girls. I will discuss these ideas in more detail in Chapter 11.

Educational strategies aside, a key point to notice is that Mrs Thomas's printouts and screenshots of those 'private' conversations and images are not difficult for her to access and print off. So one can easily imagine how much easier it is for the police to do that and be able to trace and unearth even more evidence. Such evidence can come from many formats and methods that bullies use, such as fake blogs, Facebook pages, pseudo identities, secret second phones, criminal threats, offensive messages, fraudulent activities (such as creating Facebook pages under someone else's name) and hate messages.

SEXTING: THE TAKING AND DISTRIBUTING OF SEXUAL IMAGES ONLINE

Mrs Thomas also spoke of sexting problems at her school. The taking and sending of indecent pictures of children is an offence. In one particular case, where two teenagers had fallen out and ended their relationship, the boy had then distributed an indecent picture to his friends that his ex-girlfriend had taken of herself and sent to him. But it wasn't only the boy who found himself facing a potential criminal record. Both were cautioned for their actions under the Protection of Children Act 1999 because the girl had taken and distributed the picture. If a young person is charged and found guilty of sexting, at the very least it is likely to result in a caution; but it could also lead to a criminal charge that places the perpetrator on the Sex Offenders Register. There is even the possibility of a prison sentence.

PROSECUTING CHILDREN, YOUNG PEOPLE AND PARENTS

As we have seen, it's not only children's involvement in cyberbullying that the law seeks to address; it can also seek the prosecution of adults, bystanders and even victims who seek retribution. For example, it is not unknown for parents to join in. Let's imagine that two girls who attend the same school become engaged in bullying behaviour online; one the bully and the other the victim. The victim tells her mum but, rather than deal with the issue calmly and getting the school involved, she becomes engaged in aggressive communications directly with the bully. Then the bully's mother gets involved and the whole thing escalates as vitriolic comments are exchanged. When incidents such as this take place, the parents can also become embroiled in the investigation and may find themselves prosecuted for harassment and abuse.

Bystanders too can get involved simply by passing messages on and 'liking' posts or supporting them in other ways, such as adding a smiley or thumbs-up icon. This too can attract the attention of prosecutors. Finally, victims of bullies who've decided to try to get revenge through the power of technology may well find themselves prosecuted for doing so.

HOW ACCEPTABLE IS IT TO PROSECUTE CHILDREN?

So far in this chapter I've discussed how and in what circumstances the law can act when cases of bullying are uncovered. But now let's ask ourselves an important question: is prosecuting children and young people always acceptable? As we've just seen, sometimes the perpetrator may have been the victim of bullying in more traditional contexts; a victim who is hoping to get some retribution through the perceived distance that online bullying appears to offer. After suffering months of face-to-face bullying at school, without reporting it, and with no evidence to prove her harassment, she's had enough. On a Friday night she sits down in front of her computer. She turns it on, takes a deep breath and creates a fake Facebook account.

She feels safe, and a huge sense of relief that she is finally doing something about the situation to help her feel better. She has a sense of power and distance as she types – because, after all, it's not the 'real world' and it's much better than doing nothing. On Monday morning, she looks forward to going to school for the first time in what seems like a lifetime; she actually wants to be there, wants to see how her former adversary is taking it.

As she walks into the playground she sees that finally she has the attention of the teachers. They're all looking at her. She also has the attention of the police. She's led to the head teacher's office where, laid out on the desk, is the evidence of her 'work' in the form of a printout. Finally the system is working: someone has been bullied, and it's been taken seriously. Very seriously. The irony, of course, is that someone who has suffered for months gets the blame. She shouldn't have done what she did, but we can understand why. The system has failed her: why didn't her teachers pick up on what was going on and make an early intervention? She felt isolated and abandoned and took what seemed to her to be retributive justice, but it backfired. Cases like this show just how important it is to consider the wider context, the situational and systemic factors, when prosecuting certain cases of bullying and harassment. And, of course, when this is done properly the investigation should uncover not only information about the erstwhile victim's bullying, the fake Facebook account, but the extent of Alpha's long-running playground bullying too.

While investigations have their place in tackling bullying behaviour, it isn't the aim of the law to constantly bring charges against children and young people involved in antisocial behaviour. The National Police Chief's Council (NPCC) clearly states that it doesn't support prosecuting young people if it can be avoided. It would rather see children and young people supported and safeguarded through the intervention strategies put in place under the Children Act 2004. These interventions include using the law as a framework around which to build classroom activities and an understanding of what key terms (such as bullying, harassment, abuse and threatening behaviour) actually mean. One of the best ways to do these things is through discovery learning in a controlled environment where young people can explore and understand the role of the law in bullying issues and consider their own and others' behaviours in the light of what is and is not acceptable. I will discuss ways to do this in Chapter 11.

ANTISOCIAL BEHAVIOURS

Bullying, whether face to face or through technology, is undeniably antisocial behaviour. Girl bullying in both these contexts usually involves the active recruitment of supporters and the involvement of bystanders. However, the cyber context hugely increases the problem because it engages many more participants than traditional bullying. Nevertheless, both contexts give cause for concern under civil and criminal laws, and bullying in both contexts may attract the serving of a Criminal Behaviour Order (formerly an anti-social behaviour order or ASBO). The main difference between the two is that bullying via technology creates far more visible, retrievable and damning evidence, which can be used in a court of law. Looks, glares and sneers are impossible to use as evidence unless they are witnessed; words and images sent, received and forwarded online can be traced, identified and printed out.

SUMMARY

'The intent to cause humiliation, harm or distress' is present in all forms of girl bullying. The abuse of power, the misuse of perceived friendships, relational aggression, social isolation and humiliation, name calling, dissing looks and taunts, messages, images and a desire to socially destroy another person are all central elements of 'intent to cause distress'. All of these can be uncovered during a thorough legal investigation. When we approach the whole issue of indirect bullying by girls, whether traditional or online, the guidelines for safeguarding set out in the legislation give us an indication of how serious and widespread the problem is (see pages 130–132). In this way, the guidelines offer us a good starting point to identify and act on what needs to change.

While focus in the past has mostly been on the behaviour of individual bullies, we also have to fully acknowledge organisational and systemic responsibility. As we've seen, the Children Acts of 1989 and 2004, the Education and Inspections Act 2006, and the DfE's supporting guidance, *Keeping Children Safe in Education* (2015), clearly set out the legal duty of a school to protect its pupils. This means that dismissing girl bullying as normal, as 'girls being girls', or accepting a systemic ethos of bullying behaviour can be seen as a failure to protect a child. And that will leave a school facing possible legal consequences.

In order to focus on these issues, we need to create an all-inclusive definition of bullying that covers all the methods that perpetrators use, based on the legal definition of antisocial bullying behaviours. This extended definition is my contribution to that need:

> Bullying consists of a complex web of antisocial behaviours. These include physical intimidation, verbal harassment, belittling verbal and non-verbal signals, the abuse of power, flaming, threats, defamation of character, the aggressive manipulation of friendships and other aggressive actions which have the deliberate intention to cause a victim to feel distressed, humiliated or socially isolated through face-to-face methods or the use of technology. These antisocial behaviours may be carried out by one perpetrator or by many. Culpability lies just as much with those involved in supporting a bully, or with being a bystander who fails to report bullying behaviour, as with the bully herself.

PART TWO
THE WAY FORWARD:
STRATEGIES FOR CHANGE

Chapter 8

ALL IN THIS TOGETHER: A SHARED UNDERSTANDING

INTRODUCTION

In this chapter I want to pull together some ideas around developing a shared understanding for all the key stakeholders. By this I mean looking closely at the issues of conflicting definitions, ambiguous messages and inconsistent approaches to proactive and reactive strategies so that really effective anti-bullying policies can be written and acted upon. In order to do this, it's useful to think about school as an environment that includes different groups of people who should *all* be involved in the process of creating and sharing the anti-bullying ethos. The ethos can't simply be dropped on people from a great height. It can't be a top-down process where a small group of adults make all the decisions and tell all the other stakeholders what the rules and the definitions are. It has to involve all the stakeholder groups as the process evolves. The stakeholder groups are school staff, governors, parents, carers and pupils.

School-based interventions for bullying behaviours are aimed at reducing reactive strategies and increasing pro-social behaviours. In my view, this work begins with open and full consultation on the development of an anti-bullying policy. When that consultation process allows the whole school community to participate fully, there is a high chance that the policy will be effective. The full process normally includes: establishing a usable, unambiguous and realistic definition of bullying; setting out clear reporting routes so that young people have various methods of reporting an incident through which they feel that they will be listened to sensitively; incident action flow charts that map out, step by step, how and where young people and adults can report bullying behaviour; regular dates listed for future reviews of the policy that clearly show this is an ongoing process; the key leaders and coordinators of the anti-bullying process named with details about how they can be contacted; training days; and embedded classroom activities. Achieving this level of stakeholder participation and detailed information both increases the awareness of policy content and significantly enhances the sense of ownership for everyone involved. Increased awareness and perceived ownership are essential for success.

Additionally, stakeholder participation promotes the sense of individual responsibility within each group as well as at a systemic level. But I must stress that if success is going to be achieved, the consultations have to be designed in such a way that everyone feels it is safe to be honest and open with each other, that everyone can offer their views in the full knowledge that they will be listened to with respect and that their views will be taken seriously.

One of the key elements necessary for this broader involvement of stakeholders to work is a child-centred approach. For many years I have focused on listening to children and allowing their voices to be heard and included in policies and papers that affect their lives. A child-centred approach reduces the risk of anti-bullying work being top-down, out of touch and non-inclusive. In short, this means strategies, definitions and policies are developed *with* and *for* young people. As I've said previously, this approach is not simply another tick in the 'consultation process' box which means a few surveys were sent out with closed 'yes' or 'no' type questions. When a full participation consultation process is pursued, it becomes a journey of learning to share the anti-bullying ethos across all the stakeholder groups, especially the children and young people. This work requires careful organisation and planning and isn't going to happen overnight, so it's important to bear in mind that developing a shared understanding in anti-bullying work across all the stakeholders will take time and commitment.

In addition to young people, there are other key stakeholders who need to be included. All parents and carers should be offered the opportunity to take part in consultations. All teachers should be encouraged to engage, not just those who are committed to pro-social behaviours and modelling pro-social behaviours, or those who feel pressured into desperately producing an anti-bullying strategy before the school inspectors arrive. Every teacher should feel that engaging with the development of these policies is an integral part of their professional responsibilities. Only when strides have been made towards achieving this increased level of participation can a shared understanding of what an anti-bullying ethos is, and what it means, really begin to take root. Once it begins to grow and flourish, school staff need to bear in mind that any sustainable, shared understanding is a never-ending commitment that requires regular, open and ongoing consultation with everyone.

A SHARED UNDERSTANDING OWNED BY ALL STAKEHOLDERS

In order to embed anti-bullying work, we need a starting point. This begins with the formation of an anti-bullying steering committee with representatives from all the stakeholder groups who are prepared to commit to full and complete transparency. The first task is for the committee to fully own and then map out the school's current position with regard to anti-bullying work. This step needs complete honesty and rigour so that what is not working can be exposed and then conscientiously addressed. From this mapping out process, questions can be developed to put to all stakeholders in a questionnaire or survey. (You can find some sample questions in Appendix 2.) The questions will likely cover areas such as the clarity of definitions, perspectives on strategies and methods of dealing with bullying behaviour, levels of support for victims and bullies, and general feedback on what works well and what doesn't. These questions can be disseminated in the form of a survey with open questions that allow respondents to write freely about their views. Alternatively, they can be explored and debated in discussion groups. (A sample questionnaire is available in Appendix 3.) Once the responses are collated, work on developing the outline of the policy can begin. But rather than seeing the end goal as the creation of a one-dimensional document, it will be far more effective to view policy development as the first step in a process that begins to direct a journey and shape an ethos.

RECREATING A SENSE OF COMMUNITY: LEARNING THROUGH LISTENING

I recently ran a training day for school staff. The conversations turned to the notion of a school community and how the sense of community has faded over the years. Among other things, we discussed how social networking seems to have made 'friendship' something that can embrace distant relationships (where 'friends' have never actually met) as well as face-to-face ones. Some of the staff said that young people don't seem to meet up as much as they used to and that school no longer determines their circle of friends. They thought that friendship groups had become more 'replaceable' and were scattered through both physical space and cyberspace. Many believed that the size of their school and the large number of pupils was a significant factor in the fading sense of community spirit.

But then another staff member pointed out that it wasn't only the sheer volume of pupils but also the school culture, particularly the attitudes and behaviours of some of the school teaching staff, that had a negative impact on the sense of community. She and others observed that the staff often break off into groups and cliques, and that there was no real sense of staffroom camaraderie any more.

The final big talking point was the issue of teachers rewarding pro-social behaviour. They found that many students were embarrassed by it. Whether it was because the teachers were deciding what pro-social behaviour was (a top-down policy) and the students weren't ready to buy into it or own it, or whether it was because the students found pro-social behaviour unacceptable wasn't clear to the teachers. There was also a sense of uncertainty among some of the staff about publicly acknowledging pro-social behaviour at all. Whatever the case, it seems that schools have experienced a severe shift in the 'norm'. The current behaviour model seems to include both a loss of any real sense of community and a sense of shame among young people in being identified as acting pro-socially by school staff in front of their peers.

Nothing breaks down a sense of community more than the idea of division and separation, of unequal groups who don't want to cooperate in the pursuit of some worthwhile, shared purpose. Girl bullying is all about 'them' and 'us'. But as we have seen above, 'them' and 'us' is also present in some school staffrooms. The common understanding of how to behave and how to be seen to behave in order to establish a sense of community and shared purpose has become warped.

Of course, we know that we can't turn back the clock to smaller schools and staffrooms. But we can move forward. We'll need to change our thinking in many ways. Perhaps most of all we'll need to get away from top-down approaches and *include* the students in creating newer, healthier and more inclusive ways to promote shared responsibility and shared understandings that stem from their experience, their ideas and their language. An anti-bullying policy co-created by all stakeholder groups is much more likely to reach agreement on a shared understanding of what constitutes healthy behaviour and what is antisocial behaviour, including definitions of bullying. This will doubtless be a long journey, with much hard work ahead. But if we do choose to commit to it, there is little doubt that incidents of bystander apathy could be reduced, the reporting of bullying behaviours could be increased and the ownership of pro-social behaviours could be accepted (perhaps even expected), and then slowly the current unhealthy 'norm' could begin to change.

In my opinion, the place to start is to explore what the idea of a community means to young people, their parents and school staff. The only way to find this out is to ask the stakeholder groups for their opinions. Below I have given some activity suggestions.

- Adult stakeholders: carry out a survey and run focus groups to find out if and why they think the school is/isn't working as a well-functioning community. Ask for examples and use them to try to capture the essence of what makes a healthy community in today's world. Ask for suggestions on how to create more of that sense of community for the whole school.

- Young people: have open discussions in focus groups about what they think a desirable community is, and then support them in workshops to devise strategies which begin to create, or recreate, a desirable community ethos. What kind of community would they like to be part of, both for themselves and others? Use vignettes (short stories of no more than two paragraphs) that give examples of desirable, functioning communities or undesirable, non-functioning communities. The vignettes can be based around suggestions from young people about the kinds of context where they have to share spaces together. Afterwards, ask them to discuss the question, what would help you to feel part of one large school community? (There is an outline of how to run an effective focus group in Appendix 4.)

- School leadership: leadership in this context has a delicate role to play. It must lend credibility to the process and take responsibility for the outcome of the consultations, but on the other hand it must not dominate and must truly listen to the views of all other stakeholders in an egalitarian way. Activities to help achieve this community spirit need to be centred around discovering strategies that help leaders talk less and listen more, show the other stakeholders they are genuinely interested in and supportive of what they have to say, and yet be able to articulate clear ideas of their own. Leaders will need to manage a genuinely democratic process in which their own views and opinions will be open to debate and challenge. Their contributions will be offered as an equal part of a package to which many other voices will contribute in order to foster a shared understanding of how to build a community and develop the pro-social behaviours that support it.

BUILDING A SOLID FOUNDATION

After listening to the views of stakeholders on what creates a community, the next thing to do is build a solid foundation for the policy. Above all, this means generating a shared, clear definition of bullying. I offered my definition in Chapter 7, and while I'm happy with it, it isn't written in stone; it's a guide. Neither was it written for any particular school. Government definitions of bullying weren't written with particular schools in mind either, but they do have legal implications for your school which must be acknowledged. Whether you're working from my definition or the DfE's

(2014a) (which states that bullying is a repeated behaviour, carried out by groups or individuals, that can be physical or emotional, may be motivated for racist, religious or gender based reasons, and be carried out face to face or through cyber channels), both are a good springboard for your discussions on a policy that will suit your particular needs. In other words, use these definitions as a basis to create a tailored definition that embraces the statutory elements *and* the views of your stakeholders. Without working hard towards the development of a shared definition, there will be confusion and too much wiggle room for Alpha to play down her behaviour, as the following examples illustrate.

Fifteen-year-old Zoe neatly disclaims her bullying behaviour as, 'I don't bully people; I'm just a bit intimidating'. Here are three thirteen-year-olds – Kirsty, Holly and Georgia – explaining how easy it is for them to reframe their bullying behaviour into something completely normal and acceptable:

Kirsty: I don't think I'm a bully; sometimes I can be a bitch.

Holly: Yeah.

Georgia: Yeah.

Kirsty: Yeah, sometimes I can say, like, 'you tramp'.

Holly: Everyone can be like that.

Kirsty: Y'know.

Holly: Yeah.

Kirsty: Yeah.

Georgia: Well, y'know, you are a bully if you go round calling them tramps.

Kirsty: Yeah, I know, that's what I mean.

Holly: That's not bullying.

Georgia: 'Cause that could mentally disturb them when they're older; they could go all paranoid and everything.

Holly: That's their business. [Kirsty laughs] I know it's not their fault they're tramps, but …

Georgia: Everyone's a bully at some time in their lives.

(Bishop, 2003c)

Allowing young people to generate and share their views, responses and experiences of bullying is just about the most powerful, insightful, child-centred anti-bullying work that you can do. It's most effective when it includes all of the following: views, perspectives, opinions about strategies, reporting channels, how people feel they are treated if they do report and how things could improve for them. Here are a few steps you can take to help young people express their views and ideas, and to think about them more deeply.

- Use vignettes to trigger discussion of cases of antisocial behaviour in school, focusing on what they view as bullying and what they dismiss. Their views can be challenged by each other or a moderating teacher/adult to encourage them to enquire more deeply into their thinking, beliefs and perspectives.

- Use vignettes and focus groups to ask young people about their views and suggestions on the following: how reporting procedures could be improved, what different strategies could be used to help reduce bullying behaviour and how victims, bullies and bystanders can be helped to explore the choices available to them when incidents occur.

- All sessions should conclude with one person summarising the discussion and drawing together all the suggestions. This can be more effective if a young person is chosen to undertake the summary and then the whole group is asked to approve it.

- Measure the outcomes of the activities and discussions immediately through inviting the participants to fill in a reflective worksheet based on the learning outcomes of each exercise. For example:

- Describe what you think bullying behaviours are:

  > How do you think people who bully should be sanctioned?

  > How do you think people who are bullied should be supported?

  > What should bystanders do when they see bullying or read bullying messages?

  > Describe the ways that you can report bullying at school and list who you can go and talk to.

After a few weeks, return to the topic and invite participants to complete the worksheets again to see if there has been any change in their views and thoughts. New thought requires repetition, so consultations with pupils need to be constantly revisited and embedded in the curriculum. This can be achieved by lesson plans being included every term in personal health, citizenship, social development or other relevant curriculum spaces. At the same time, similar active participation work with parents and carers is likely to be equally insightful. Consulting with parents and carers on their understanding of definitions, and on their attitudes and

perspectives about bullying, are vital if an anti-bullying ethos is going to embrace the whole school community. While it's unrealistic to expect 100% support from all parents and carers, there is a far higher likelihood of increasing engagement if all parents are offered the chance to participate regularly in a range of anti-bullying consultations. Typical consultations may include conversations about the following stages in the process: where are we now, where can we go and how can we get there, as well as all ongoing consultations after that.

The outcomes and insights from the focus groups, surveys and anonymous case studies that parents agree to contribute to can support the ongoing development of the anti-bullying policy in many ways. For example, they feed into the creation of a shared definition of bullying and also establish an active commitment to the proactive and reactive strategies that form a key part of the policy. As you can see, this process will never work if it's one-off or piecemeal. It has to be an ongoing process, with consultations regularly held and the policy updated annually.

POLICY DEVELOPMENT: WHAT *NOT* TO DO

I've supported many schools to design their anti-bullying policies over the years, and I've audited far more than I could begin to count. I will now use that experience to provide my view on what constitutes a weak policy and then set out a useful outline on what makes for a stronger, more transparent and more widely owned policy that actually works. There are certain elements that must be included in any policy and which should form the backbone of that policy. These elements include relevant legislation and guidance, safeguarding requirements and school improvement commitments. It's also important to keep in mind that staff dealing with bullying issues will only find a policy useful if there are clear definitions of antisocial and bullying behaviours included within it, and that the types of sanctions applicable, and in what contexts, are meaningfully outlined. The policy should, therefore, provide support and clarification for staff when carrying out sanctions. In addition, because the policy forms the legal basis for anti-bullying action and inaction within the school, the protection of young people could be at risk if it doesn't clearly stipulate reporting channels, sanctions for bullying behaviour and what support is available for those involved.

In short, it has to be said that there are some very weak anti-bullying policies sitting on many head teachers' shelves. Here are some of the reasons why many anti-bullying policies leave a great deal to be desired.

Weak policies:

● Contain definitions that are standardised and use words that mean little to the reader.

- Are not revised each year.

- Are revised each year but without consulting the key stakeholders.

- Are too long-winded.

- Use too much jargon and complicated words and syntax; they are not reader-friendly.

- Alienate those who most need to know the contents.

- Don't involve young people and parents in their construction, beyond tokenism.

- Aren't tailored to the specific needs of the community or to a genuinely shared understanding.

- Fail to engage with the young people or parents who read them; for example, they can't remember the definitions or they don't know who to go to in order to report bullying.

As a result of these and other weaknesses, many young people are either reluctant or afraid to act in line with the policy, as they haven't been fully consulted and have therefore not understood or engaged with its aims. They remain suspicious of it and disconnected from it. This attitude is further compounded if the young people and parents have not been encouraged and supported, through effective consultation and training, to do the following: report bullying, know the channels open to them, understand that it is safe to report, know how to act to reduce antisocial behaviour and understand the responsibility of bystanders to act pro-socially.

POLICY DEVELOPMENT: DR SAM'S POLICY STRUCTURE

A model anti-bullying policy doesn't exist, for the simple reason that any policy has to be tailored to each particular school. Therefore a skeleton policy is an excellent starting point for that tailoring to begin. I have sketched out a basic framework to help and guide schools to create a policy that allows the whole community to take part in its development and to own it. An effective anti-bullying policy should include clear and succinct sections on the following:

- *Page 1 – Policy objectives:* state the aims of the policy and the anti-bullying ethos. (Remain faithful to the safeguarding commitment of the school.)

- State the *statutory obligations* of the school, including the relevant legislation and guidance concerning safeguarding commitments, with particular regard to bullying issues.

- Clearly state the agreed *definitions and strategies* developed throughout the consultation process – in particular, the definition agreed and signed up to by the whole school; an outline of the various methods of bullying, including bullying of or by staff; and a clear statement of reporting channels which reflect a whole school approach to seeing and reporting.

- *Page 2 – Marketing of the policy:* list how you will make the policy easily accessible, child-friendly, parent- and staff-friendly (for example, through printed leaflets, the school website and the use of anti-bullying activities throughout the year).

- Include clear statements of *intervention strategies* for victims, bullies and bystanders (both reactive and proactive). This can be done using concise bullet points.

- *Page 3* – Provide a simple flow chart for *resources*: for example, senior leadership roles, named anti-bullying leads in school, the anti-bullying lead governor, supportive clubs, groups, external partners and referral routes.

- *Page 4* – Set out clear guidelines on how bullying *data and the recording of outcomes* will be gathered: for example, a statistical summary of reported bullying incidents; pupil perspectives on how often they have been bullied; and levels of pupil, parent and teacher satisfaction about how the school deals with bullying incidents.

- *Page 5* – *Consultation process*: clearly set out who the participant groups will be, the timeline of the consultation process and the range of methods to be used, such as classroom activities, focus groups and surveys. Include the annual review date.

The table below is an example of a simple way to show summary details of the ongoing consultation process throughout the year. It also gives reference points for curriculum management of the anti-bullying work and of the wider participation of the whole school community.

Stakeholders	Summary of involvement in policy development	Date of activity
Pupils	Termly focus groups: part of curriculum activity on anti-bullying topics Peer support training throughout Year 7 Termly assembly presentations Anti-bullying week, focusing on definitions of bullying Year 9 visit Year 6 of feeder school to explain the buddy system in place at the secondary school	
Parents	Focus groups Survey participation Annual consultation for policy review Invitations to anti-bullying week assembly	

Stakeholders	Summary of involvement in policy development	Date of activity
Teaching staff	Termly curriculum work Annual anti-bullying training in school Annual anti-bullying training out of school Inter-staff focus group participation Effective listening training sessions in school	
Support staff and lunchtime supervisors	Annual anti-bullying training in school Annual anti-bullying training out of school Inter-staff focus group participation	
Governors	Annual anti-bullying training in school Inter-staff focus group participation	
Anti-bullying committee	Annual policy review as agreed by the committee	

Here are a few suggestions to keep the policy current and user-friendly:

- Aim to keep the policy to six pages or fewer.

- Update annually with legal requirements, and state the date that this will happen.

- Keep it alive in the eyes of the whole school community and in full view by placing it on the school website and making it an active part of school life throughout the year.

- Always have a child-friendly, parent-friendly and teacher-friendly policy on the website.

SUMMARY

Developing a shared understanding of bullying and bullying issues means that adults can help young people by supporting them to actively engage in the process of creating an anti-bullying policy. This engagement gives them greater ownership of their lives and reduces the ambiguity that has traditionally tended to surround the definition of bullying.

Taking the decision to create a whole school anti-bullying policy also shows a commitment towards the building of a shared ethos. I believe that open consultation through a variety of different methods is where this process should begin. While the change to an all-encompassing anti-bullying policy will take time, incorporating the views of all stakeholder groups is vital. Without a thorough, inclusive consultation process it is unlikely that there will be any real ownership of the policy, and therefore a very limited application of it. The policy has to belong to everyone in order for it to be effective. And to be effective, it has to be written in an appropriate way so that each group of stakeholders can engage and identify with it. The policy must be easily accessible and usable.

Developing an effective anti-bullying policy is just the beginning. Once it's written, revising it should be an ongoing process. If it is left untouched and unvisited, life in the playground will revert to the law of the jungle and the old, undesirable 'norms' will return. All the hard work will be forgotten. On the other hand, if it's kept at the forefront of everyone's attention in daily life, through the establishment and maintenance of expected behaviours in classrooms and the playground and through ongoing activities in school, and kept alive among the stakeholder groups in various ways, then there's a good chance the anti-bullying ethos will gain a shared understanding and a strong sense of ownership. And if pro-social behaviour is regularly reinforced, with the consent and validation of all stakeholders, it is much more likely to become embedded and normalised.

Adult stakeholders (teachers, parents and carers) are responsible for developing policies that safeguard young people and positively influence their time at school. An effective anti-bullying policy should develop a sense of self-worth and safety at school for all the students. Ineffective policies, on the other hand, are hardly worth the paper they're written on. Their vagueness, inaccessibility, exclusiveness and other limitations frequently contribute to a sense of daily dread for far too many children.

Chapter 9
DEVELOPING REPORTING CHANNELS: EVERYONE'S RESPONSIBLE

INTRODUCTION

Adults risk contributing to the damage that young people suffer from bullying when they fail to listen or respond to their pleas for help and intervention. Every time this happens, young people's faith in the adults, and the authority they represent, can be shaken or even shattered. In this chapter I want to suggest some ways to improve reporting systems and consider how to develop some trust in them, because I've lost count of the number of children and parents who have said to me, 'What's the point of telling? No one listens.' And sadly, they're often right.

In order to change this situation, we need to find ways to let young people know and feel that they really *are* being listened to, that they are being heard and taken seriously. In order to do that, we'll need to make the reporting of bullying incidents everyone's responsibility.

We'll also need to consider the process of bullying, which usually falls into two stages. The first stage is the immediate harm caused by bullying actions on the victim. I call this *primary damage*. In earlier chapters we saw how this type of damage impacts on an individual's psycho-social, cognitive and personality development; in particular, the areas of self-esteem and self-concept. There is also a second stage. *Secondary damage* can be caused whenever there is a failure to respond in effective ways when bullying is reported. This is particularly true when reporting is denied, dismissed or not taken seriously.

Secondary damage happens when a young person who has been bullied, seen bullying or heard about an incident reports it to an adult who, for whatever reason, fails to sensitively listen or effectively act. The result can be long-term damage to psychological development. Faith and trust are diminished and the young person's sense of self-worth takes a battering. In addition, the feeling of not being listened to, and the perceived sense of unimportance or invisibility, leads to a further reduction in reporting. This not only affects the young person who has made the report but also those on the outside – the bystanders, peers, parents and, of course, Alpha herself – who all see and note the lack of action taken.

It's not surprising that many young people involved in bullying incidents, whether as victims or bystanders, begin to think, 'Don't bother seeing it, don't bother telling anyone. What's the point? Just ignore it and let it all become invisible.' So let's be clear. The key to encouraging reporting, and discouraging bystander apathy, begins with the development and implementation of a trusted and robust reporting system.

BREAKING THE CODE OF SILENCE

If we're to tackle bullying effectively we can't avoid coming face to face with the wolf pack. At some point bullying has to be challenged directly. The best way to do that is through an effective reporting system. The power and ferocity of Alpha and her pack only increase in the absence of an effective anti-bullying ethos and reporting process. Alpha relies on an ineffective reporting system. It allows her to intimidate and threaten those who dare to report her behaviours. Fear of reprisals from Alpha mean that it is safer for victims and bystanders to not report and remain silent. It is the line of least resistance. In Chapter 5, I outlined how Alpha's intimidation leads to a code of silence which generates a perceived, though fragile, sense of safety among pack members and bystanders. This code of silence means not betraying Alpha, whether one is a pack member or an out-group member. In this way, little by little, the code of silence becomes embedded, a not talked about part of the whole bullying culture. So, one of the biggest challenges we face is: how do we break through that code of silence?

The first thing we can do is to use the open discussions on anti-bullying work that were discussed in Chapter 8 to highlight the reporting channels available when antisocial behaviour occurs. Second, we need to make it crystal clear that reporting is *everyone's* responsibility. It's not just the victim's problem. Third, we need to recognise that Alpha's direct threat is only part of the equation. The other part is poor reporting systems and procedures.

In my view, the issue that most undermines people's willingness to report bullying incidents is when reports are heard but not sensitively dealt with. This is compounded when adults use words that come easily but are not followed through with actions. For example, when school staff make statements like, 'If you don't tell us, we can't help you', and then fail to do anything meaningful when a young person actually does tell them about bullying. No wonder they feel that no one is really interested and that no one is prepared to help. 'What's the point? Why bother?'

In the UK, as we saw in Chapter 2, the police have a motto which they use in the context of developing greater social awareness: *Notice, Check, Share!* It aims to invite and motivate the public to become more aware of antisocial behaviour. First of all, *notice* it. Then *check* that what you see is what you think you see. Finally, *share*, tell and report it, based on a clear sense of right and wrong, of what is acceptable and unacceptable, and what constitutes healthy and unhealthy social behaviours.

I want to apply the same motto to girl bullying, so that children and young people can see how making a report in a well-constructed and sensitively organised reporting system can make a genuine difference. Here are some suggestions for a starting point using classroom-based activities in school:

- *Notice* – Classroom work to identify bullying behaviour. Use storybooks and puppet shows for younger pupils, or soap operas for older ones, to show examples of bullying. Then invite them to list, verbally or in writing, all the bullying behaviours they noticed in the scenario.

- *Check* – Follow up with an open discussion of each character's behaviour in the scenario. What exactly did the bully do or

say? What were the behaviours of the bystanders? Now refer the students to the school's child-friendly anti-bullying policy (see Chapter 8). Allow the children and young people to identify for themselves how the school community has agreed to act when bullying occurs. This is best done in small groups to encourage everyone to contribute. Follow this up using feedback from the groups in an open, whole-class discussion. Be sure to ask some probing questions such as, 'What could or should you do if you see bullying behaviour like this in our school?' and 'How will that improve our school community?'

- *Share* – Now focus on the reporting channels in the policy. Ask which reporting channels students can identify. This can either be done in small groups that report back to the whole class, or it can be done individually as a written activity. In the latter case their responses could be anonymous; the staff member then reads them out to stimulate group discussion.

The responses from these exercises can become a springboard for follow-on activities: rewriting a script for the soap opera; helping younger children to put on their own puppet show; writing a short story; using drama to improvise or act out pro-social behaviours that would usefully challenge the antisocial ones. These activities should demonstrate an awareness of the roles of everyone involved, including bystanders, plus references to reporting channels, expected outcomes and what to do if someone reports but feels that no one is listening or taking them seriously.

The *learning outcomes* of these activities could include reinforcing a shared understanding of what bullying is; promoting clear definitions of bullying; understanding that being a non-reporting bystander serves to encourage further bullying; establishing exactly what the reporting channels are and how to access them; and raising everyone's awareness that reporting is their responsibility. Activities such as these are very rich in their application. The students' work, especially that generated by the creative processes of debate, writing and drama, can form part of the ongoing consultation process for the whole school approach to anti-bullying. Allowing them to engage directly in this kind of discovery learning generates a sense of ownership of the anti-bullying work and embeds the new learning in their minds. The material can be logged and fed into the ongoing policy reviews as part of the young people's input. This is not, of course, a one-off process. The work needs to be embedded by returning to it and reinforcing it every term.

MULTIPLE REPORTING CHANNELS

In order to reduce the risk of young people feeling that no one will listen to them, attention has to be focused on developing a *sensitive listening system*. Let me say first what this *doesn't* mean. It doesn't mean taking hours out of a school day to sit for long periods of time with just one child. Nor does it mean sitting in a tranquil and softly lit environment with Mozart playing gently in the background. In an ideal world this may be OK, but it is completely unrealistic for most settings where bullying occurs and where staff are multitasking and very busy.

It's not the environment that needs to be perfect; it's the response and attitude of the listener. Warm, caring and sensitive always trumps cold, dismissive and rushed. Of course, busy professionals are often under pressure to get things done and pay attention to many things at once, so caution is required. Sometimes it's just not possible to listen to a child's initial report in more than a cursory way. When this happens, a clear promise must be given to sit down with that child later in the day to help reduce any feeling of being ignored or unimportant. Turning a child away without acknowledging the importance of their experience, and without setting a clear time and place to hear them out properly on the same day, may well result in them never coming back. Any perception of lack of acknowledgement can lead young people to feel that they are in the wrong for reporting. It takes an awful lot of courage to report, particularly when pro-social behaviours are not yet fully embedded into the school culture.

To improve reporting channels, it's usually necessary to have multiple reporting channels based on the needs of young people and parents. These can include:

- Guaranteeing anonymity by using a *bully box* for pupils or parents to report issues; they can put their comments on pieces of paper and post them in the box anonymously.

- Using a school map exercise. This is a simple yet powerful activity where students express how they feel in different locations around the school. A simple map of the school and school grounds is made and distributed. Students then place emoticons (sad, OK, happy, etc.) about how they feel on different parts of the map. This helps staff understand which locations may be prone to bullying activities, and also where students feel safer. Instead of emoticons, colour coding or

numbers can be used. For example, 1 means very safe or happy and 10 means very anxious or sad. These maps can be named or anonymous. You could hand out stickers showing a mobile phone icon which pupils could place on the map *outside* the school to indicate any bullying that is occurring beyond the school boundaries and outside school hours. You could also include a box at the edge of the map listing all the available reporting channels.

- Making a listening service available to all students, ideally at the same time and place each day. This is really effective when it is a buddy or peer support system run by the students themselves, who provide the service and then liaise with school staff using a package of support. Of course, the students will need to have been trained in supportive listening and safeguarding skills so that they know when they need to refer incidents to a member of staff. The space will need to be somewhere quiet and away from the normal school traffic.

- Choosing the best location for the support room. Use the maps described in the mapping activity to determine the places in school where young people feel safest. These are the locations where reporting is most likely to happen. Locate the support room, and access to peer support, buddy systems and other anti-bullying services, in these areas. Further discussion with pupils will elicit the reasons for the sense of safety these locations offer which can provide additional useful information.

- Offering a page on the school's anti-bullying website as a location where bullying can be reported. Writing is easier for some young people than face-to-face spoken interaction.

- Devising a special school bullying app to help young people access the reporting system with more confidence. Many schools have used this strategy with great success.

- Making the time and effort to embed a whole school community approach so that everyone is on the lookout for antisocial behaviour and everyone knows it's their responsibility to notice, check and share.

- Providing regular training for every member of staff on how to respond to each bullying or reporting event using sensitive listening skills.

- Placing posters in every school corridor, in changing rooms and on toilet doors. These posters should show a clear flow chart of the various ways to report bullying, and the names of those heading up the anti-bullying teams on the school staff and school council.

- Ensuring a feedback form is available for every person who reports, whether parent or child, on how well they felt they were listened to. Have a dedicated team in place to follow up on this feedback.

SENSITIVE LISTENING

The success of an effective and trusted reporting system depends on two factors: the quality of the staff response to reports, and whether the reporters feel listened to or not. There's a big difference between talking *at* someone and talking *with* them. There's a big difference between hearing the words and listening to the anguish beneath the words – letting the young person know that their distress is really being acknowledged. Creating a listening environment that allows young people to feel safe and really heard isn't quite as easy as it may seem. A safe physical space is important, but much more important is the psychological impact of a quality interaction.

Many adults feel the need to speak for young people; for example, by filling in the words the reporters are struggling to find for themselves or by finishing off their sentences. Although the intention may be good, the effect is not helpful. In short, they are putting words into their mouths. They are disempowering them by taking away their struggle to name and own their reality. Instead of giving young people a voice, many adults are taking it away from them by being over-solicitous. Here are a few suggestions to overcome this.

- Don't be afraid of silence. It's just thinking time and encourages the reporter to find the words they need.

- Don't require a young person to look at you when they speak. Face-to-face talking can be intimidating and confusing as the reporter searches their visual, auditory and emotional memory banks to recall what happened. They need to find the right verbal and non-verbal ways to express their experience, and if they have to face you while doing this, they may find your non-verbal responses distracting.

- Give the reporter time to speak. To listen, all you need to do is be quiet and pay close attention. Rather than finishing off words and sentences, offer signals of support and interest. Invite the speaker to continue by saying things like, 'Yes, I understand that you're saying …' (sometimes repeating the exact words used by the reporter can help if it doesn't further upset them; if it does, then rephrase gently but retain the meaning). Or offer a gentle 'yep' or nod of the head to show you are engaged and listening and that it's OK for them to carry on speaking *and* thinking.

- When the reporter has finished, repeat back a summary of what they have told you. Ask if there is anything else they want you to know.

- Help young people to overcome the barriers that often accompany talking about feelings. If you ask directly how the bullying has made them feel it can sometimes block a conversation and make it awkward for the reporter to find the right words. Feelings aren't easy to put into words, especially when emotions are raw. So direct questions about feelings can not only be difficult but will often make victims, in particular, feel more exposed and vulnerable.

One method I use to get around this problem is a rating scale. I draw a scale of 0–10 and, rather than lock eye contact with a child, I point to the scale and clearly explain 0 is the lowest and 10 the highest: 'So, on a scale of 0–10, 10 means you feel very sad most of the time at school because of the bullying, 5 means you are sad sometimes and you're OK sometimes too. And 0 means that everything's good. Now can you point to where you think you are?' You can also use colours or emoticons to do the same with younger children. Having done this and allowed the reporter to commit to a spot on the scale, it's much easier to now open up a discussion with them. The scale works as a distraction from face-to-face immediacy and encourages a conversation about emotions.

- Ask the young person what they think could happen next, especially in reference to the anti-bullying policy that they have helped to develop.

- Let them know what you will do next.

- Reassure them about when you can meet again and what to do if the situation needs immediate support.

Our aim as sensitive listeners is to allow the young person to feel listened to, and not judged or intimidated. Above all, we need to help them feel empowered. Here are some tips to help you achieve this – and some pitfalls to avoid.

- Don't use tick box exercises to record incidents. Such activities lead to quick-fire, closed questions that only require yes/no answers which don't allow a young person to speak or a listener to hear what needs to be said and understood. Tick boxes limit conversations and focus on gathering data alone. We should be exploring data *and* feelings.

- Using formal phrases such as 'witness statement' can be unhelpful because they raise the stakes. Unless the incident leads to a police investigation, such terms are usually inappropriate. Replace formal language with more conversational terms such as, 'What's your perspective?', 'What's your view?', 'Let me know what you saw'. This keeps reporting much more child-friendly and less scary, and encourages a conversation to expand rather than close down.

These are strategies that help both listener and speaker to have more engaging, real and helpful discussions.

Listening to parents and engaging them in the anti-bullying process requires exactly the same approach. This means the use of everyday language, allocation of time to listen properly, the employment of listening skills that enable them to feel heard and clearly established, times and dates for further discussions or meetings. If a parent-friendly, whole school community policy has been established and embedded, this will be an incredibly strong foundation on which to base meetings and to support the development of a shared understanding. Unless these parameters are in place, meetings with parents can turn into a battleground where little or no agreement can be reached on anti-bullying issues or the types of behaviour that can be classed as bullying. When this happens, any shared understanding of a way forward is unlikely to take place.

KNOWING WHO TO TALK TO

When I work with troubled young people, one method that I frequently use to help them know who to go to if they need support is called the *helping hand*. It's a simple yet powerful strategy to help them remember who to call on for help when they need it. It uses a mnemonic based on an outline of their own hand. This is how it works:

- Ask young people to draw an outline of their hand. Younger children can cut out the drawing if they wish.

- Now ask them to think about adults in the school community who they feel they can trust and talk to. Invite them to choose the four they trust most and ask them to write a name on each of the four fingers. On the thumb they write the name of a buddy or a peer supporter.

- This 'helping hand' is their personal support team. It's a team the child can call on at any time and around whom the child can feel safe.

- Younger children can make a display of the hands for the classroom wall. Older children can keep their drawing in their school diary, desk or locker. Review the children's 'hands' regularly by asking them to say who is on their helping hand, whether or not they are still happy with the 'team' and if there is any name they wish to change.

This activity not only helps young people to identify an accessible support team that they can go to whenever they need to, but it also reduces their reliance on just one person, who could be away from school just when the child needs to talk to them. This strategy allows the child to take responsibility for creating their own named team, rather than having a top-down approach where the support group are nominated by the school leadership. The list is also a clear indication of which people are influential in that young person's school life and the individuals they feel they can really trust. That's incredibly rich and useful information that might be difficult to obtain from a conventional interview.

Sometimes a young person can struggle to complete the task, and that too is telling. If that happens, slow down the process and ask them to talk through the names they *could* put on the hand and why those people belong in their support team. Don't force them to complete it. Let them know that it's worth them having a little think about it over the next few weeks and maybe they will be able to think of someone else they would like to add. Then return to the activity at a later date. This leaves the door open for further chats.

A genuine support system plays a huge role in developing a young person's confidence. Faith in the system, and the kind of trust that comes from being able to talk to adults and be deeply listened to when help is needed, is the foundation of this confidence. This also holds true for the development of confidence across the whole school community. I have spoken to staff and parents who have tried to report bullying but felt they haven't been adequately listened to. Staff and parents need to know who to go to for support just as much as the young people do. In fact, there's no reason why the 'helping hand' can't be used in a slightly adapted form with staff and parents too.

As was discussed in Chapter 8, an effective anti-bullying policy should clearly map out the routes available for reporting incidents of bullying and include named contacts for parents and staff to talk to. The reporting channels for all community members have to be made clear and be accessible, and the quality of response to all reports needs to be sensitive, reassuring and robust enough to offer confidence in the system.

REACHING OUT BEYOND SCHOOL FOR HELP

Sadly, no matter how much we would like the reporting of bullying to lead to effective interventions, it isn't always the case. Girl bullying causes serious psycho-social damage and sometimes it's necessary to involve external agencies in the support network. These can include psychological, clinical and educational support services; mental health services; behaviour management interventions; and family services. The issues that some girls face, whether as bullies or victims, simply can't be supported by school staff and it's necessary to refer them onwards for further intervention. In my opinion, all adults should be focused on safeguarding issues and on the option of referral to external services if necessary.

Staff have sometimes told me that they feel referring a bullying issue to external services represents a 'failure' to solve a common problem. Rather than hold this negative view, I suggest that referral should be viewed as a 'thumbs-up' that they understand and recognise the impact that girl bullying can have, and that it demonstrates a clear commitment to fully supporting each child with the best help available. In this context, it can be very useful for adults to make their own 'helping hand' to remind them of their own support team, whether peers, leaders or others. A useful adaptation is to pop 'external services' in the space provided by the thumb. It's really helpful for adults to remember to share the responsibility, not feel alone when dealing with bullying, and – above all – not to try to do everything by themselves.

SUMMARY

Shared responsibility and individual responsibility are both a huge part of an effective reporting service. *Notice, check, share* is a good motto to remember, primarily because it reminds us that it's everyone's responsibility to report bullying and other antisocial behaviour. Those who are tasked with listening to the reports of children who are bullied or who are bystanders have a social duty of care to listen sensitively, discuss constructively and act effectively. If that duty is acted on, we can genuinely hope to have a positive impact on a child's belief that the system will support them, that seeking help from others can be worthwhile and, at its very best, transformational.

While not all reports will be supported by evidence, and some will prove not to be genuine, staff always have a duty of care to listen and act sensitively. Clearly, school staff are busy people and may not be able to deal fully with a report at the time it is made. In such cases, time should be made to initially *hear* the report, establish that it is a matter of genuine concern and then set a time later the same day when reporter and listener can sit down together and exchange what needs to be shared. The existence of realistic goals and clarity about the availability of reporting channels is essential to this process. In developing an anti-bullying culture and ethos, sensitive listening and effective action empower young people to speak up more often and with greater confidence. On the other hand, failing to listen disempowers young people and leads them to distrust the system and remain wary of using reporting channels.

A well-constructed anti-bullying policy that is friendly to children, parents and teachers alike forms the basis for all actions that can be taken to tackle issues as they arise. These include *where* a report can be made (for example, the support room location), *how* a report can be made (the various reporting channels that are available) and the responses given *when* a report is made (the quality of the listening and questioning). I have suggested various activities and strategies to begin this type of work and encourage each school and staff member, and of course the students too, to add their own suggestions and ideas for further activities. Above all, it's essential that the process has the full support and engagement of the whole school community.

Chapter 10
BUILDING HEALTHY RELATIONSHIPS

INTRODUCTION

The ability to make friends is something that many of us take for granted. It's also something that most adults assume is a skill that young people possess. In most cases that's true: young people can make very healthy and successful friendships based on honesty, trust, support and mutual respect. On the other hand, girl bullying thrives on unhealthy friendships and abusive social relationships. In this chapter, I want to explore ways to help young people recognise the differences between healthy and unhealthy friendships, and how to improve their friendship-making skills.

Friendship-making skills begin to develop at a very early age but can be damaged at any time in childhood by unhealthy interactions. In Chapter 2, we looked at how the sense of self emerges as children progress from toddlers to teens and also how that self relates to others as children grow and mature. In the playground, a child has to make decisions about how to fit in and who to try and befriend. They soon learn that having a friend or two is a necessary and desirable thing. In order for us to understand the drive that young people have to build friendships, we have to pay attention to what influences young people's social relationships, how they choose who to walk hand in hand with and also why they think they're chosen as a friend by others. In essence, we need to know what friendship means to them in order to begin to disentangle healthy from unhealthy friendships.

The starting point for this understanding comes from talking with and consulting young people and trying to look into their world. The next step is looking at their role models – the people who influence them, especially in the ways they manage their friendships. Interventions for girl bullying need to focus on clarifying the underlying nature of young people's social relationships. Then we can develop strategies to help them learn that mutual friendships enhance relationships, whereas conditional friendships damage their self-esteem and sense of self-worth. The damage caused by conditional relationships is frequently carried forward to future unsuccessful relationships in adult life.

If we're conscious and aware of these things, we can use the classroom and the playground as effective learning environments for supporting young people to develop constructive social relationships. Tackling the negative impact of unhealthy friendships is not easy, but it is possible to guide young people towards developing healthier social interactions if we educate them about the more positive choices they can make.

CLASSROOM AND PLAYGROUND MANAGEMENT

Options and choices are generally something that some young people who have been bullied don't understand. They've been disempowered and had their self-esteem battered so many times that just being accepted by anyone is all they hope for. And this is exactly what Alpha needs in order to manipulate them. How they have come to such a state of isolation and low self-confidence is a complicated mixture of life experience and behavioural patterns. These might include shyness, lack of social skills, being seen by others as different and negative relationship models. Turning around this lack of confidence isn't straightforward, but it generally begins by adopting a culture of inclusion across the school community. This supports the development of an ethos based on everyone making the effort to ensure each person's voice is heard and respected, and each person taking responsibility to consciously include everyone in the social process at all times, rather than just sometimes or not at all. This shared commitment is an integral part of building any effective anti-bullying ethos. Without it the ethos is tokenistic and simply won't work.

Building this ethos begins with adults modelling a culture of inclusion and conducting healthy relationships between each other and towards young people. It's not realistic to expect every adult to be a role model to young people at all times. After all, adults have emotional and relationship issues too. But it is realistic to expect most adults, when they are around the children in their care, to demonstrate what a healthy relationship is and how to manage conflict in productive and diplomatic ways. If this doesn't happen, young people will lack the guidance they need. Many will take this as an endorsement that it's OK to scream and shout, to never apologise or compromise or to refuse to forgive or resolve conflicts in gracious and conciliatory ways.

It's perfectly normal, of course, that from time to time young people will experience the breakdown of a friendship, or get too close to an unhealthy relationship, or be treated without respect, or even be the one treating others like that. Support and guidance in social relationship management is essential so that young people can learn strategies to deal with such eventualities, and this requires adults to constantly model the 'do as I say *and* do' attitude. Parents and school staff are crucial in influencing young people's behaviour. We are all immersed in social relationships all the time, whether as father and daughter, teacher and pupil or support staff and head teacher. The more respect, mutual listening and genuine caring shown by adults, the better. The more adults demonstrate that power games and social manipulation are unacceptable, and that pro-social behaviour is not only expected but desirable, the better the chance that young people will adopt an inclusive culture in the classroom, in the playground and beyond.

A good starting point for building a culture of inclusion is an open discussion about when and where young people feel empowered at school by staff and peers and when they feel disempowered. Discussion of this topic can generate some surprises, so be prepared to talk through these issues. This can be uncomfortable but it will provide steps from which to move forward. For example, adults in particular need to model the following behaviours:

- Make sure everyone's point of view is listened to and heard.

- Apologise if you make a mistake or regret your behaviour.

- Be prepared to let go of an argument and move forward without constantly referring to it.

- Don't humiliate or embarrass others.

- Don't shout at others if you think they have got something wrong or if you disagree with them.

While the points on this list may appear to be very obvious, take another look and consider ways that some staff members or other adults may ignore these basic guidelines. All social relationships set a benchmark for others. It's not acceptable or workable to have one rule for adults and another for young people. When these agreements are in place, the culture of the classroom will be much more conducive to cooperative learning and to the constructing of a respectful environment in which pupils take mutual responsibility for managing and negotiating effective social relationships.

HEALTHY RELATIONSHIPS

Developing a healthy relationship allows a child's self-worth to grow and flourish. They feel wanted, needed and worthy. But this can only happen when young people learn to recognise what a healthy relationship is. We therefore to find out what they think a healthy relationship is, and we can only discover this by speaking to them. While carrying out research for this book, I asked fifty-eight girls aged from eight to fifteen to list some key words that they felt described a 'good friend'. Here are some of the terms they used, with percentages of frequency: trustworthy/loyal/honest/keeps secrets (53%), kind (45%), caring/understanding (34%) and makes you laugh/funny (21%). Other answers included: helpful, happy, has good manners, supportive/helpful, respectful, doesn't hurt your feelings, doesn't pick on you, listens, always there for you, doesn't slag you off/call you names and has same interests. I also asked them what they thought made a 'bad friend'. Their responses were: (people who are) disloyal/untrustworthy/dishonest/tell secrets/ two-faced/slag you off (80%), call you names/say mean things/ bitchy/spread rumours (33%), physically hurt you (28%) and mean/nasty (10%). Other answers included: swears, steals from you, disrespectful, uncaring/unkind, selfish, uses your friendship, mardy, blackmailing, leaves you out, tries to control you, tries to change you, secretive, never there for you, hypocritical and sly (for the complete data set, see Appendix 1).

This type of information can easily be gained from the following activity, which can be done with young people of all ages:

- Ask them to list anonymously what they think is important in a friendship. Collect the lists and collate them.

- Then discuss all of the terms they've used, and their meanings, with the whole class, asking them for examples of these behaviours.

- Now flip the positive friendship traits around to look at their opposites – for example, trustworthy/untrustworthy.

- Work with the pupils towards a shared understanding of healthy and unhealthy friendships. Make sure you include an exploration of how a healthy relationship can make a person feel and the same for an unhealthy relationship.

- In small groups, ask young people to discuss and list how they could be a 'good friend' to someone. Then invite feedback and discussion across the whole class that establishes a shared meaning of what makes a good friend.

- One week later, run a creative follow-up session to embed the learning. This can include relationship-building games; making posters; writing songs, poems or stories; creating soap opera scenarios; drama activities such as freeze-frames and role plays; and writing scripts about making healthy friendships.

- Present this work in assembly and create displays around the school.

DEVELOPING PEER SUPPORT SKILLS FOR ALL

Peer support provides a mechanism for students to help each other in the school context. At its heart is the co-operation and friendliness natural to human beings.

(Cartwright, 2007, p. 10)

I worked with ChildLine for three years studying the training that young people received to become peer supporters in school. In the extract below, fifteen-year-olds Claire, Steven and Anne told me

(Sam) how they go about helping pupils whose self-esteem has been damaged through bullying:

> Claire: We have another thing called validation which we do …
>
> Steven: Mmm …
>
> Claire: … which is when they come in and say, 'Ah, nobody likes me, I'm so horrible, everybody hates me', and then you say, 'Well, *I* like you' and we say everything [positive] about them. And then we do self-validation when we make them say what's good about themselves, which is for helping them with their confidence.
>
> Anne: It can also break behaviour patterns because there's the theory that everyone's born nice and everything, like. Ninety-nine per cent of the time we're behaving in a behaviour pattern, and when in the past if we were crying someone might have stopped us crying, so now we think we're not allowed to cry …
>
> Sam: Mmm.
>
> Anne: … but if we talk about it, you get to play it in your mind and you can wipe it …
>
> Sam: Mmm.
>
> Anne: … and forget about it and …
>
> Sam: Mmm.
>
> Anne: … and it's really good when you stop a behaviour pattern because then you feel you'll be better.
>
> (Bishop, 2003c, p. 100)

At this point, I have to add the caveat that self-esteem is not quite so easily increased, and behaviour patterns are not quite so easily changed. But I do remember clearly that these young people had a deep understanding of the negative impact that indirect bullying has, and a belief that the damage can be reversed if early intervention by peers takes place. This awareness of supporting others to feel better about themselves is a life skill that is an essential part of an inclusive culture.

Peer support training offers the acquisition of many such life skills. I have argued for years that training a group of young people to be peer supporters is incredibly valuable, both for them and for the school. But wouldn't it be even more valuable to train *all* pupils in peer support skills, thereby offering them excellent social skills for life? This training could be integrated into slots for personal, social and health education. Skills training for peer support includes listening skills (as discussed in Chapter 9), validation techniques (as described above), safety strategies (offering clear boundaries for peer support, safeguarding issues and referral to staff), talking about and understanding feelings and emotions (as explained in Chapter 9 using the 1–10 scale), dealing with feelings and emotions (in particular through using vignettes, drama and role play) and problem-solving and conflict resolution skills.

Here is one suggestion for how to approach and discuss conflict resolution:

- In small groups, ask young people to discuss what healthy and unhealthy friendships are and then write down key words for each of the two categories.

- Write 'Healthy' on one side of the board and 'Unhealthy' on the other and invite the whole class to add their key words for each category.

- Discuss the words openly and be sure the meaning of each word is clear to everyone.

- Now ask what 'conflict' is and generate a shared understanding of what it means.

- Work through all the words in the 'healthy' relationships category, asking what happens when conflict occurs in those relationships. Then invite students to share constructive methods and strategies that can overcome conflict and offer effective solutions.

- Now do the same for the words in the 'unhealthy' relationships category. Work through the solutions, but be prepared to spend a lot more time on this section discussing why it's more difficult to sort out conflict in unhealthy relationships. As this becomes clear to the students, emphasise that strategies exist that will effect more positive solutions.

- Place all the suggested strategies into relevant categories – for example, rekindling friendships, building empathy, agreeing to differ, agreeing to move forward and leave the past behind, setting goals about how to move forward and agreeing not to flame, harass or humiliate.

- Finally, ask the class how these suggestions can become part of how they help to resolve conflict in school.

- One week later, follow up with creative story-writing exercises which include constructive conflict resolution.

These are excellent activities for dealing with conflict and support-ing young people to find ways to resolve it. However, there's another area that's closely related to conflict which challenges some young people – and quite a lot of adults too – and that is how to handle the inevitable, and often very powerful, emotions that can surface when working with girl bullying.

EMOTION VS. EQUILIBRIUM

On more than one occasion I've been asked how to deal with girl bullying without talking about emotions. Three of these requests came from maths and physics teachers; all of them were from men who wanted to find ways of dealing with girls and bullying without getting caught up in the emotional talk that inevitably accompanies these issues. And while I have nothing against keeping emotions out of explanations, I have to say it's really difficult to keep emotions out of girl bullying. However, while I was looking into cases of girl bullying, including cyberbullying methods, I began to think about the evidence trail that bullying leaves and the impact that long-term conflict can have on young people. I began wondering how a young person's awareness of this long-standing impact could be used as a tool for behaviour change. So, to see if that would help, I turned to John Nash's game theory and the more recent adaptation of its use in conflict resolution. John Nash was the distinguished economist and mathematician whose work was made widely popular in the film *A Beautiful Mind*.

Game theory is the study of strategic decision-making. According to game theory, helping a person work successfully through a deci-sion-making process is based on their understanding of the options available to them and then weighing up the risks that accompany the choices they make against the costs on the one hand and the benefits on the other. Saaty (2008) extended Nash's theory and applied it to non-cooperative situations in major international conflict. Although bullying isn't quite international conflict, it can certainly feel like it for those trapped in the middle. I'd like to teeter on the edge of Saaty's work and think about challenging the ways that perpetrators, bystanders and victims think about their behaviour by getting them to work through a process similar to that outlined above. Depending on circumstances, these activities can be used as a one-to-one process with perpetrators and victims, and as a group activity with bystanders.

Use questions like the following to help young people take a step back from their reality and do some 'bigger picture' problem-solving about their current situation and where they might want to be in the future.

- What can I actually achieve with my behaviour as it is?

- What might my current behaviour cost me?

- What do I want to achieve in my life this year, in two years' time, in five years' time?

- How much influence will my behaviour have on me in the long term?

- Will my current behaviour be effective in helping me to succeed in school, in life and as a friend? Or will it stop me being successful?

- What do I need to change? What do I need to do differently?

- Starting today, what plan can I make to help me begin to change that doesn't seem too scary?

Ask the pupils to draw up their answers as a list of pros and cons about keeping or changing their behaviour.

Now you can try the following activity or adapt it to suit your circumstances. When working with an alpha female, the process might go as follows.

Ask her to write down a list of the short- and long-term gains she might achieve from *continuing with her current behaviours*. The list might include:

- I like the impact of my behaviour – it makes me feel powerful.

- I like getting others to do what I want.

- I like my strong public profile; I like being seen as powerful by others.

- I have a high social status through standing up to authority and being able to manipulate others.

- I impress people and they want to be around me.

- I don't get hurt because I don't show my feelings.

- I am brave enough to say exactly what I think.

Now discuss with Alpha what might happen if she thinks about the consequences of continuing with her antisocial behaviours. Then ask her what could happen for her present self and future self *if she chooses to act, and be seen to act, in healthier, more pro-social ways.*

Ask her to write down all the short- and long-term benefits that might come from changing her behaviour in this way. The list might include ideas like these:

- I feel proud that I can make choices about my behaviour.

- I can reduce the level of conflict in my life.

- I can increase my problem-solving and conflict resolution skills.

- There's less likelihood that my online profile will prevent me achieving my goals in life (e.g. if I want to go to university or get a good job).

- There'll be a higher chance of me having unconditional, trusting, loving relationships in my life and having real friends.

- I'll see evidence of my new pro-social behaviours and social contributions on future CVs.

The gains can be placed on a timeline, beginning with short-term strategies for change and then going on to show mid- and longer term changes. Any initial changes need to be viewed as small steps or else there is a risk that the cost will seem too high and too difficult to achieve.

Activities like these, which encourage young people to explore the consequences of their behaviours and how these behaviours can have a seriously detrimental effect on achieving what they desire, offer a powerful resource to support ongoing positive behavioural change.

In psychology we're often looking out for the 'imbalance' that occurs when the current behaviour of an individual is unlikely to support them to achieve their long-term goals and desires. We call the gap between the two *disequilibrium*. Often disequilibrium is accompanied by a thought process along the lines of, 'I don't know how to change', 'What's the point in changing?', 'I can't stop her doing this to me, so what's the point in you telling me how to act and what to do?' Game theorists, as well as psychologists in general, work towards solutions that establish *equilibrium* instead. That means helping individuals who want to achieve their desired short- and long-term outcomes create and own the necessary changes in their behaviour, so achieving them becomes more likely. While I can't promise this approach and these activities will completely circumvent the possibility of emotions arising, it could help to provide a more objective framework for those who prefer that approach.

CASE STUDY

Building a culture of inclusion: *James and the Dragon*

At the age of nine James became a victim of relational aggression, bullied because he loved to dance: just like Billy Elliot. His distressing experiences at school included being the target of social isolation and humiliation by his peers. James began to withdraw from social life and even from his family, but finally he found a focus. He started to think about the thousands of other children who had been victims of relational aggression, and he found a way to try to stop it happening. In 2009, at the age of twelve, James became the youngest person ever to appear

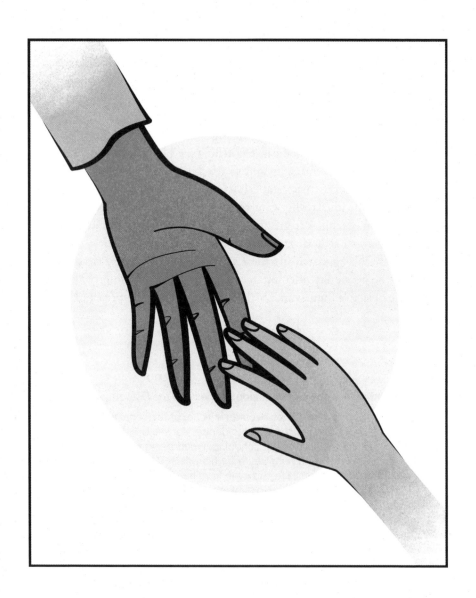

on the TV programme *Dragons' Den* (as part of an episode for *BBC Children in Need*).

On the programme, James presented his blueprint for challenging relational aggression in primary schools. The idea he devised rewarded pro-social behaviour through stickers, and weekly awards given in assemblies, to children who had looked out for any child who was lonely or isolated and included them in their games and circle of friends. He called his business idea 'Look for Loneliness'.

While appearing on TV could not have been easy for a nine-year-old, James stood tall for such a little chap. When challenged by some of the dragons that the system already existed, he robustly defended his case. As a result, two of the dragons, James Caan and Duncan Bannatyne, offered him the amount he had requested. They then asked James to make a choice. Would he prefer to take half from each or choose just one of the dragons to invest the total sum? After some thought, James very politely showed how much he truly understood and practised pro-social behaviour. He thanked Duncan for his kind offer but accepted the investment from James Caan. When asked by Duncan Bannatyne why he made that choice, he smiled and said, 'I really like James as a new dragon and wanted him to feel welcome'.

In fact, the system that existed in many schools was not at all about others seeking out lonely or socially isolated children. Instead, it required victims of bullying to find the courage to identify themselves and either stand under a sign or sit on a 'friendship bench' and wait for someone to come along and sit next to them. How humiliating is that? While we want to find ways to empower children to seek support and resolve problems for themselves, this ill-conceived strategy is like telling them to walk around with a sandwich board that says, *Have a good laugh; I'm Billy no-mates.*

James recognised those issues. By the age of eleven he had written a collection of children's books promoting his idea that social integration is everyone's responsibility. I've had the great pleasure of knowing James and his family for many years now, and I can confirm that he has become a confident and focused young man who is on his way to becoming a professional performer.

EMPOWERING YOUNG PEOPLE

I also know that James's mum and dad were often driven by empathy for their son; his hurt was their hurt too. It is, of course, only natural for parents to want to protect and defend their child, be they victim or bully. But rather than snatching the problem off the child with the intention to safeguard and protect, it's usually a much better strategy to work through possible solutions with them. Inviting a bullied child (or a bullying child, for that matter) to talk through problems is often given little credence and is therefore undervalued. But actually it's the first key step in putting the young person at the centre of a problem-solving exercise. It requires the young person to vocalise the problem and their feelings, and then make sense of their experience. This is essential if we are to support children to begin empowering themselves. After this first step, follow-on discussions allow them to explore further ways of moving forward.

I have worked with many distressed young people, and one method that I often use with issues like relational aggression is to use a series of questions like these: 'Let's begin with how you feel about telling me this so you know it's OK to feel the way that you do. Let's look at what's making you feel like this, what's happened and when.' And then I'll prompt them through that structure; we normally both end up with a much clearer idea of what has taken place. Only then can we start to think together about some of the ways we can try to move forward.

Strategies like these empower young people to take greater control over the situations they find themselves in and allow them to take greater control over their resolution. As a result, they begin to develop life skills that enable them to deal with conflict, friendship issues and relational aggression, not to mention exploring a whole variety of options and strategies for when life gets tricky. It's amazing to see how their social skills and personal confidence can develop. When an anti-bullying support team works with young people and their parents, all parties feel more empowered and feel that they have greater control over challenging situations. That's what successful anti-bullying work is all about.

SUMMARY

For young people to build healthy relationships, they require positive adult role models that show them the way forward. Young people need support to be able to value themselves, and a key component of this is being listened to and respected by adults. If they don't value themselves, how can they expect others to value them? Adults can help to create or destroy self-worth and self-esteem through the way they treat young people and the way young people see them treating each other. The importance of modelling on young people's lives and relationships reminds adults that they have an important role to play in helping to set a standard for what is and isn't healthy and acceptable in relationships.

A shared understanding of what constitutes respectful and healthy relationships has to be built, to which young people, parents, carers and school staff can all buy in and commit. That shared understanding will dramatically improve the chances of developing an inclusive culture in the classroom and playground that supports young people to negotiate conflict, work with and through emotion, and turn around unhealthy and antisocial situations. Dedicated curriculum time needs to be set aside for this work as it can empower young people with life skills that can protect and strengthen their sense of self-worth and self-esteem, as well as that of others, just as we saw in James's story.

Chapter 11
MANAGING CYBERBULLYING

INTRODUCTION

When I deliver staff training days on girl bullying, I can guarantee one of the first topics that will be raised is cyberbullying. That's because staff are struggling to cope with it. Girl bullying has two extremes. At one end of the scale there is face-to-face bullying, for which it can be difficult to find hard evidence; while at the other end of the scale there's reams of evidence for cyberbullying in the form of printouts from phones, tablets and computers. Staff are increasingly spending large amount of time reading through these screenshots and feeling overwhelmed by the sheer amount of information that cyberbullying generates, and staff frequently say they feel at a loss about how to begin to tackle it. I'll let Mrs Thomas, who we first met in Chapter 7, explain how many of her days begin: 'I've got evidence here today and it's screenshots of what's gone on … it's continual.'

In Chapter 6, I explained my view that cyberbullying is a method of bullying rather than a separate type. Incidents don't need to be treated differently from face-to-face bullying. If they are, it encourages young people to compartmentalise antisocial behaviour as being somehow different depending on whether it's on- or offline. It also leads staff to feel unnecessarily confused. They overcomplicate things, so they're often struggling to find strategies to tackle cyberbullying rather than keeping it simple.

In my view, there needs to be much more joined up thinking to bridge the perceived divide between face-to-face anti-bullying strategies and those applied to cyberbullying. When a more cohesive approach is developed, there is much less confusion about what is and isn't antisocial behaviour on- and offline, and a much greater recognition of the similarities in intent and impact of antisocial behaviour both in the real world and in cyberspace.

The roles and methods used by cyberbullies reflect pretty much the same roles and methods used in traditional girl bullying. For example, the alpha female can manipulate and influence her pack to engage in online bullying behaviours in much the same way that she organises and orchestrates their antisocial behaviour in the playground. Often she'll carry out cyberbullying acts in full view of pack members – at a sleepover, for example – or she might encourage her pack members to do it on her behalf. On the other hand, she might act alone because she knows she's guaranteed an audience online, an admiring audience that she craves, just as in the playground.

Or perhaps it isn't Alpha bullying online at all. Perhaps it's Omega wanting to taste some of the power of those above her in the hierarchy. This may seem different to the playground scenario, where Omega would never behave in this way, but the point is that the methods and the intent are the same. As we saw in Chapter 6, she can do it because she thinks she can protect herself by using the anonymity of a pseudonym, or a second mobile phone, or a false social media account.

As we've seen, the screen gives a false sense of security to those who want to harass and humiliate others. It removes the sense of direct contact with victims and offers a false idea of distance, which diminishes all sense of personal responsibility. This distancing effect also gives bystanders the impression of being less complicit in incidents and, as such, they are less likely to report them.

All strategies to tackle these issues, whether proactive or reactive, will need to take these factors into account if they are to be effective. But we must not lose sight of the bigger picture: the perceived sense of distance doesn't alter the fact that the intent to bully, and the responsibility of others to challenge and report antisocial incidents, are really no different from what happens in other forms of bullying.

As adults, we need to accept that the world is different these days and that the social world of young people is part virtual and part real. It's a world where a great deal of communication and interaction happens on the screens of phones, tablets and computers, and where text messages are viewed as conversations. These texts, otherwise known as Short Message Service or SMS, make it easy for those copied in to add emoticons or quick comments that can add to the impact of the message. When the message is antisocial in intent, this extends relational aggression at the press of a key.

Proactive strategies are required to challenge cyberbullying and create long-term change. This can best be achieved through education, in particular discovery learning, which allows young people to research and discover the facts for themselves. This allows for a bottom-up approach to learning which supports them to own and act on the new information. Topics for discovery learning could include definitions of bullying; bullying and the law, with particular reference to any intent to harm, harass and humiliate others;

the reach of the school's anti-bullying policy; the school's 'acceptable use' of IT policy; and the long-term social consequences of bullying.

CREATING PROACTIVE INTERVENTIONS 1: LISTENING

When I first thought of writing this book, I wanted to consult with young people and let their voices and views be present throughout. Part of my research focused on what they thought about cyberbullying, and I was interested to find out how they viewed it. Was it something completely different from traditional bullying or not?

I listened with great interest, and also with some shock and surprise, to what over seventy girls in my survey and focus groups, aged between eight and fifteen, had to say about the cyber-world in general. The first thing that became clear to me was that they see the cyber-world as the centre and anchor of their social life. Without it they would have very little social life outside school. In Chapter 6, I reported that a girl called Becky had asked, 'What would happen if we didn't have social networks?' To which the answers were, 'I wouldn't go out 'cause I'd have no social life' and 'I'd just watch TV'. These thirteen-year-old girls make it clear that they see social network sites as being the portal to their social life and an escape from routine and boredom. That escape includes becoming involved in online interactions, even if that means joining in with bullying interactions.

This suggests that many young people feel a strong social need to engage in online communication, both as an avoidance strategy for boredom and also for developing a sense of belonging to social groups that can link them back to the world of school and beyond. Thirteen-year-old Kirsty goes further, though, suggesting that the desire to engage and belong may also attract her to the power and shelter that comes with affiliation to the pack mentality: 'If there's an argument on Facebook I have to get myself involved 'cause I'm bored and have to make a comment. I just comment with a laughing face and get called a bully. But [I'm] not, it's just a laughing face. I just like to read through the comments.'

These comments help us to recognise the centrality of the cyberworld to young people and – for some of them – its importance to their sense of social status and social identity. But I also gained more insight about what happens when cyberbullying is seen as separate from, and even completely disconnected from, traditional bullying. When I asked girls who were taking part in the 'Do I Look Bothered?' project to describe to me how girls bully, these were the responses they gave: 91% said that bullying was done verbally, face to face; 9% said it was done through cyberspace; only 2% mentioned texts. For these girls, 'bullying' was generally understood as a face-to-face experience. If it wasn't face to face, most of them didn't consider it as bullying. In my view, this compartmentalising is the most serious thing that needs to be addressed and redressed if we are to successfully tackle the issue of cyberbullying. We need them to connect cyberbullying with more traditional forms of bullying so they can see that they are really the same.

The focus groups I worked with taught me a lot about how young people view cyberbullying. The following are some of the key themes that emerged as salient in young people's understanding, misunderstanding and general confusion about what is or is not online bullying. These themes help to form the basis of a new understanding of how and why young people get involved in cyberbullying, and why they seem not to know where the boundaries lie between what is acceptable and what is unacceptable online behaviour. Above all, there was confusion over the following four themes:

> *The right to reply:* 'What if you're having a go at someone on Facebook because they've had a go at you?'
>
> *Power relations:* 'What if you both got into an argument?'
>
> *No brake pedal:* 'But, like, when you want to say something, you have to say it.'
>
> *Is this good or bad?:* 'If there's an argument on Facebook I have to get myself involved ... we were sticking up for that person. They [the teachers] said we were bullying ... and the school got involved [but] we were only sticking up for them. Is that bad?'
>
> Or, 'I saw a guy on Facebook and he had his xxxx hanging out and someone took a picture and posted it on Facebook. I felt sorry for him. [But] if you get it and send it to someone, is that bad?'

The themes show how useful focus groups can be when a child-centred approach is used in the development of anti-bullying strategies. Focus groups can provide very rich, and often surprising, information that helps us explore the issues more deeply with them; issues that we may not have been aware of without such opportunities to deeply listen to the reality of the young people's world.

CREATING PROACTIVE INTERVENTIONS 2: FOCUS GROUPS AND DISCOVERY LEARNING

One of the big challenges when managing focus groups of your own is how to do it without taking a top-down approach. It's important that adults don't set the agenda. Boronenko et al. (2013) listened carefully to young people's views on what they really wanted from research into cyberbullying. The activity below is based on Boronenko's findings and is designed to support young people to explore issues of understanding and dealing with cyberbullying for themselves. It's also based on my own conversations with young people and listening to them telling me what they really want to be able to do.

- Ask the group to create a clear definition of what cyberbullying is, including consequences and effects.

- Ask them to discuss and decide what inappropriate behaviour is.

- Ask them how they could include their parents in work on cyber-safety, such as how to use Facebook, how to report cyber-abuse and how to work with privacy settings (in particular, understanding how they work and what protection they actually give).

- Ask them how they can help adults to understand the impact and importance of the ways children and young people cope with cyberbullying.

- Ask them how they can create strategies that increase communication between students and parents.

- Ask them to come up with strategies that allow young people to feel that it's OK to talk about experiences of cyberbullying in order to support those who are victimised.

- Ask pupils to create strategies that help parents give greater support and better advice to their children.

It can sometimes be useful to invite support staff, rather than teaching staff, to facilitate these kinds of activities. This may allow young people to be more open and less guarded. Whatever you do, my strong suggestion is that you don't focus on cyberbullying without first giving young people the time and space to clearly establish for themselves what cyberbullying is.

Follow up on this first activity within a week with another that invites small groups of pupils to research cyberbullying websites and learn what the laws are. Particularly helpful websites are:

www.gov.uk/goverment/publications/preventing-and-tackling-bullying

www.bullyinginterventiongroup.co.uk

www.anti-bullyingalliance.org

In small groups, preferably of three or four students, hand out the following list of topics and ask the pupils to research and write a paragraph on each summarising the main points, consequences and learning. Point them in the direction of any additional resources and materials they might need.

- The legal consequences of being involved in cyberbullying.

- The right of the police to retrieve messages, images and communications that have been deleted.

- The right of the police to trace messages and their senders (even when the sender thinks they are anonymous).

- The government can rule that a person's internet or instant messaging account is closed down if they are found guilty of committing online antisocial behaviours.

- The school has the legal right to read messages and investigate cyberbullying incidents.

- The school's anti-bullying policy states what action the school will take when cyberbullying is reported.

- The school's anti-bullying policy states what action the school will take if they suspect a pupil of cyberbullying.

Once the research has been completed, the students' new awareness and learning can be presented in assemblies throughout the year in the form of plays, poetry, creative stories and poster displays. A particularly powerful technique is the tableau or freeze-frame, which invites the audience to interpret what is happening and what could or should happen next. It's also really useful to invite outside speakers into school, particularly the local police, who are usually very keen to support these strategies.

LINKING CYBERBULLYING TO THE SCHOOL'S ANTI-BULLYING POLICIES AND STRATEGIES

Naturally, all this work needs to link directly into the school's anti-bullying policy, behaviour policy and 'acceptable use' of IT and mobile phones policy. With particular regard to cyberbullying, the following will need to be made very clear to students and staff:

● The rules for the use of mobile phones in school.

● The sanctions that staff can take if the rules are not adhered to (including the school's right to access messages and pictures).

● The rules on confiscation.

● The consequences that may occur if pupils resist or refuse to comply with the school's policies.

A member of the anti-bullying team at one school I've worked with in the north of England wrote to me explaining the changes they had made to reduce mobile phone use and cyberbullying during school hours.

Up until recently, the school allowed phones during the day but they were not allowed in lessons. If they were used without permission, they would be confiscated by the teacher and returned at the end of the lesson. [However,] this was not having a [sufficiently] detrimental effect on student behaviour. In addition, there were issues with students misusing mobile phones to bully others by recording/filming others in humiliating situations with the view of humiliating them on social media. In light of all this, the school decided to ban mobile phones from 8.30 a.m. until the end of the school. Students can use them during lessons under the direction of a member of staff if it is

for learning purposes. To indicate this, we have signs in class saying [whether] phones are allowed or not allowed. If students use phones without permission, they have them confiscated for the evening and get them back the next day at break time. If this happened on a Friday, they get the phone back on the Monday. In order to support students whose parents need to contact them, we provide them with an old-fashioned mobile for the evening which has basic communication features.

This top-down strategy has been very effective at this particular school in reducing the number of videos, pictures and messages taken and sent during school hours. The actions and sanctions that will be taken if students fail to comply is a clearly stated element of the school's mobile phone policy.

WORKING DIRECTLY WITH CYBERBULLIES

Rather than being quick to judge and label bullies and bullying behaviours, it's far better to look first for the reasons that lie behind the antisocial behaviour of bullies. This is because there are so many different bullying profiles and reasons for bullying. For the same reason, it's best not to react too quickly with the application of top-down sanctions, but instead to work with each bully or cyberbully to untangle the story that lies behind whatever has been happening. In order to achieve this, you'll need to get to the bottom of the following issues:

- Is this person a traditional playground bully who has extended their repertoire into cyberbullying, or someone who *only* resorts to cyberbullying?

- What is the *back story* (the often unseen or untold story underneath surface appearances) between the perpetrator and victim?

- What is the *scale* of the problem? Is it a one-off incident? Is it a campaign against one particular person? Or, more seriously, is it an embedded antisocial behaviour that has been used many times with different victims over an extended period?

- Have the antisocial messages in question been sent to many recipients, just a few or just one? Were they written in front of others (the pack) or were they written alone with no real-world audience?

- Have multiple cyber methods been used (for example, texts, blogs, instant messaging and social media)?

- Does the perpetrator's online profile show major differences to their real-life persona? For example, are their bullying actions online the result of their inability to bully face to face due to their lack of social or physical power, lack of confidence or lack of social skills? Have they themselves been bullied, and are they seeking revenge or redress?

- Is the perpetrator attempting to seek retribution for herself or for someone else?

- What does the bully intend to gain from online or telephone bullying?

Without the information that this kind of enquiry brings, dealing with a cyberbully is like catching a slippery eel with your bare hands. It's almost impossible; they just wriggle their way out from between your fingers. You need to know the specific reasons why each individual engages in online bullying. This enables the issue to be addressed so that the behaviour can then be challenged and changed. By viewing cyberbullying as an extended method of bullying, you can use all the traditional approaches to girl bullying that we have explored so far, while also recognising the role that the virtual world has played in the incident.

Helping young people to understand their own role in cyberbullying is imperative. But it's only the beginning of trying to get them to change their behaviour. Adults need to follow this up by supporting them to find ways forward that they can learn and put into action. The following is one way to influence and guide such a behaviour change:

- Get to the bottom of what has motivated the incidents and why.

- Ask the perpetrator if she has ever known what it feels like to be bullied.

- Discuss if she knows what a trusting relationship is.

- Help her to open up to you, and to believe there are options and choices she can make to change her behaviour.

- Explore together what these options and choices might be.

- Support her in learning to deal with conflict and to use conflict resolution skills (as discussed in Chapter 10).

- Discuss the gains the perpetrator feels she achieves through cyberbullying, and then gently begin to help her weigh up the potential short- and long-term gains and losses that might occur if that behaviour continues (for example, building satisfying long-term relationships, the fact that universities can check social networking site activities and incurring a caution or criminal record).

It can also be very useful to work with a perpetrator's parents, including them as part of the team to support the strategies for intervention. This allows the parents to feel fully involved and also to become more aware of the consequences of cyberbullying behaviour.

HELPING VICTIMS OF CYBERBULLYING RECLAIM THEIR LIVES

The ways to support victims of cyberbullying are really no different from the ways outlined in earlier chapters to support victims of traditional bullying. These include an open and trusted reporting system, a shared understanding of clear definitions of bullying behaviours, the ready availability of a child-friendly anti-bullying policy that clearly demonstrates that cyberbullying is an issue which will be taken seriously and tackled rigorously, even if it happens out of school hours and a clear 'acceptable use' policy for all electronic communication which is rigorously enforced.

When these strategies and agreements are embedded in the anti-bullying policy, the behaviour policy and the school ethos, and understood and agreed by all parties, then it makes sense to encourage young people who are being cyberbullied, or who are witnesses of cyberbullying, to do some or all of the following:

- Report to a trusted adult.

- Report to a networking site (for example on Facebook or Bebo there is an option to report abusive content).

- Ignore the message and not reply.

- Save the message and either show it or forward it to an adult who will support you.

- Forward examples of bullying to the sender's Internet service provider (ISP).

- Block the sender's number.

- Be aware that all message logs can be traced.

- Be aware that online abuse and threats are a matter for the police. No matter how low level you may wish to keep any abuse, you need to know when you must refer it on.

- Work through a decision-making process with someone from your 'helping hand' team (see Chapter 9) and make sure all the team members are kept up to date with the strategies that will be used.

As I explained in Chapter 10, supporting a victim of bullying means having a meaningful and focused conversation with them that encourages them to make decisions and choices of their own that help them move into healthier social relationships. These decisions and choices give back a sense of control to the victim and raise their sense of self-worth and self-esteem. But how long the journey will take can be hard to say, as it depends so much on the individual concerned. In just the same way as when we're working with bullies, we need to discover as much as possible about the victim's personality profile and the background to the bullying.

With bullying in general, and cyberbullying in particular, it can feel to a victim as though the whole world has closed in around them and that there is no escape available; no sanctuary. Their social world, both on- and offline, appears to collapse and they see no way out. In such cases, our role as adults is to work closely with the victim to help them regain a sense of control. Here's one way to kick off this process through a one-to-one discussion:

- What effect is this having on you at school and at home?

- How else is it affecting you?

- Can you think of three things that we can do together to help you?

- How can you help me to put those into place?

- What can we do in the next week to help?

- What can we do in the next months to help?

- How can you use your own IT skills to begin to manage some of the problems?

- What else can we do to help you feel more supported in social networks online and offline?

- Can you help me think of three more things that might help to stop this behaviour or situation from happening again?

- Let's write down as many ideas as we can think of to help you if any of these things do happen again.

SUMMARY

Thinking about bullying in a more joined up way, and treating cyberbullying as an extension of girl bullying rather than something completely separate, helps us deal more effectively with the issues behind it and reduces the tendency of both adults and younger people to compartmentalise it. Dealing with cyberbullying is never going to be straightforward, but it really isn't much different from the issues that present themselves when dealing with face-to-face bullying. In my opinion, interventions need not be hugely different from those used for traditional bullying, but they do need to be extended, given the nature of the technology and its impact on distance and responsibility. All interventions need to take into account the profile of each perpetrator, as well as the impact that the distancing effect has on bystander behaviour.

The law is just as pertinent to cyberbullying as it is to more traditional forms of antisocial behaviour, perhaps even more so. This is because there is some very specific legislation about the use of technology to harass, humiliate, threaten and intend to cause harm to others. Both perpetrators and victims need to be offered quality support in making choices and decisions. Perpetrators also need to be aware that evidence of bullying can remain online for many years and may create serious problems for their life choices in the future. Support work on these issues and the short- and long-term consequences of antisocial behaviour can be instrumental in influencing young people towards sustainable behavioural change.

From time to time reactive strategies and other top-down approaches will need to be taken, particularly when a serious incident occurs. However, by themselves reactive strategies are unlikely to bring about lasting change. Instead, we need to focus on proactive work that is centred on the young people involved, that promotes discovery learning through a variety of hands-on discussions and activities and which is far more likely to bring about long-term behavioural change and consequently a reduction in cyberbullying.

Helping all young people to understand the differences between pro-social and antisocial online behaviours is far better achieved through discovery learning than top-down lessons. Supporting those directly involved in cyberbullying incidents can be managed by activities and conversations that help them to take ownership of solutions and their own behavioural changes. Such strategies include exploring with them the underlying factors and implications of their back story, as well as helping them develop useful techniques, such as motivation skills to help them change their behaviour and conflict resolution skills. Further reinforcement of proactive strategies for reducing cyberbullying can be achieved through pupil presentations in assemblies and through poster presentations displayed throughout the school.

Chapter 12
A NEW VISION OF LEADERSHIP

INTRODUCTION

Leadership structures are an essential element of governance in our society. At the top of almost all social hierarchies are leaders. A healthy leadership style promotes and delivers strategic planning for the best long-term outcomes of the whole community. In many schools today there is a general appreciation that it takes a team, not just an individual, to lead a school; that team is generally known as the senior leadership team (SLT). Ideally, the SLT consists of altruistic yet pragmatic individuals whose energies are focused on delivering the best outcomes for the whole school community. In short, they care about the needs of the community they serve.

In previous chapters I've discussed both individual and institutional responsibility. I've argued that it's the role of every school to support young people who perpetrate, are victimised by or become bystanders to bullying behaviours at school. In my view, every member of the school community is part of the problem if they don't stand up and raise their voice against bullying and report any antisocial behaviour to a trusted adult in a position to do something about it. But all of this responsibility has to start somewhere. To ensure an ethos of anti-bullying is genuine, viable, sustainable and embedded across the whole school community, all anti-bullying work needs to begin with the focused determination and passionate commitment of the senior leadership team.

The SLT is the foundation upon which anti-bullying work is built. If the foundation is weak or poorly assembled, one cannot expect the edifice to stand much pressure. Nor can the SLT succeed if the strategies they implement are purely academic, window dressing or never truly tested with rigour and determination in the cold light of day. The SLT's role is to function in much the same way as parents in a family. They are there to be the backbone of school life and to ensure that the pupils' welfare and well-being are rigorously safe-guarded. They should be, and clearly be seen to be, committed to the support and empowerment of *all* school family members.

In my view, for the SLT to play an effective role in anti-bullying work it has to embrace *collaborative* leadership. Where there is collaborative leadership in school, there is no fear of transparency or reluctance to encourage whole school participation in anti-bullying work. Instead, the leadership team is fully focused on engaging the whole school community in every aspect of anti-bullying work.

School staff, as well as the SLT, have a leadership and quasi-parenting role embraced by the umbrella term *in loco parentis*. In order to be effective and respected throughout the school, community staff, supported by the SLT, need to ensure that consistent and fair responses to all bullying incidents are applied. This allows young people to feel safe in the knowledge that clear boundaries, strictly applied sanctions and effective strategies are in place to support them, and that whoever they turn to at school will listen to them and act quickly and sensitively to resolve their issues. The consistency that comes with the implementation of an effective anti-bullying policy, conscientiously applied by the SLT and staff, also reduces any risk of confusion or frustration that pupils and parents may otherwise feel about what bullying is and what needs to be done about it.

In my experience, schools with the most effective anti-bullying ethos are those schools with the most committed and supportive senior leadership teams. The key to success seems to be a combination of a leadership team that values collaboration, participation and listening, and a consistent approach to anti-bullying work shared across the whole school community. On the other hand, I've seen plenty of schools with plenty of problems in their implementation of anti-bullying work. The main reasons for failure are lack of support and commitment from the SLT, inconsistent approaches from leadership and staff, lack of shared understanding between all parties, misunderstanding and miscommunication between staff, parents and pupils about what bullying is and an anti-bullying policy that only the handful of senior staff who wrote it are familiar with.

I've heard so many complaints about schools from parents and pupils, and the commonest themes are about lack of consistency, breakdowns in communication and failings in community collaboration. One mother said to me, 'What's the point? School won't listen. The head teacher denies it's bullying. The head of year begins to help [but] then it all stops. For months I've tried every member of staff that I can think of to ask for help. I've got no choice now other than take her out and find another school.' This parent's daughter was being bullied, and the mother had lost all faith in the school whose duty it was to safeguard her daughter and prioritise her welfare. Social isolation and a loss of confidence threatened her daughter's studies and her sense of self-worth. Her daughter had lost all faith in adults helping when she had reported the bullying and found that nobody was prepared to listen.

The SLT is the glue that holds the school's reputation together. How it responds to incidents of bullying can make or break that reputation.

ACT AND BE SEEN TO ACT: AN EFFECTIVE ANTI-BULLYING ETHOS

All hierarchies necessarily have gradation. Some individuals are at or near the top, others are at the bottom and some in the middle. And, of course, there's an interesting parallel here with the 'pack' ranking and organisation of Alpha through to Omega. In schools the hierarchy extends from the chair of governors and the head teacher, through the SLT, to the teaching and support staff. But unlike Alpha's unilateral accession to power, school leadership roles are interviewed for. And in truly collaborative and transparent leadership systems, members of the whole community have the opportunity to participate in the selection process.

I've known schools in which a strong sense of community exists, where pupils have sat on interview panels for the selection of their new head teacher. Wouldn't it be useful to have a similar selection process for appointing members of the SLT? In particular, interviews for the anti-bullying lead (AB lead) and deputy AB lead? A pupil interview system will highlight who is respected by the community for their commitment to anti-bullying work, thereby strengthening the role and status of the AB lead and their deputy. The SLT then has a much stronger base on which to build a truly community supported and sustainable anti-bullying ethos.

The importance of the role played by the AB deputy is often not fully appreciated or recognised. The AB deputy ensures that the AB lead is not left unsupported, and ensures that someone will be there for the young people if the lead is away from school for whatever reason. Without a committed and energetic deputy, AB leads can become incredibly isolated, with a consequent danger of becoming stressed or overwhelmed by their workload, especially when there is little or no back-up from the SLT in general. A not uncommon consequence of this is the onset of desensitisation to bullying incidents or the downgrading of reporting – especially when it comes to girl bullying.

Power is an inevitable part of leadership. Healthy power is no bad thing, but it's always important to constantly monitor the power dynamic of any leadership team. This can best be achieved through regular meetings with all elements of the whole school community. To avoid SLTs becoming, or being experienced as, detached from the rest of the community, it's essential to maintain this type of close collaboration. In this way, school leadership is not only regularly assessed by those within the team but also by everybody who has a direct stake in the quality of that leadership. As Sherer (2008) argues, excellent leadership requires followers to participate in a successful power dynamic. *Participation* is the evidence of a healthy power dynamic. It empowers the whole community and embeds the leadership system within it. There is little chance in a system like this that leadership can retreat into an ivory tower or act unilaterally.

A review of the benefits of a collaborative school culture has been carried out by Dickerson (2011). The research suggests that a collaborative culture is important to underpin efforts at school improvement. Schools, like other organisations, can strongly resist changes to deeply held beliefs, practices and norms. For example, girl bullying is too often seen as 'normal' by senior management in some schools. Even when new staff arrive and challenge that norm, their views can often go unheard and so have no bearing or influence on policy. Similarly, some parents view girl bullying in exactly the same way. They remain resistant to the calls of other parents for change. However, when the practices of a collaborative culture are adopted and embedded, challengers are much more likely to be heard, and therefore influence policy, because the channels encourage the practice of constructive listening and open debate.

To monitor how well a school is working collaboratively, consider:

- Does the school have an anti-bullying policy that includes full participation and open consultation, including survey and focus groups, throughout the whole school community?

- Are there regular and open discussions taking place on 'leading by example' that highlight incidents of healthy and unhealthy role modelling throughout the school? These discussions can be driven by feedback from staff, parents and pupils in anti-bullying surveys and focus groups. Such discussions help to develop a norm of talking about pro-social behaviour in the open, which can help to change and influence behaviour in practice.

- Is cooperative learning adopted and implemented in all classrooms?

- Is there a flexible approach to staff appointments, and are representatives from across the whole school community included on the interview panel?

WHEN LEADERSHIP IS SEEN AS DETACHED: NEGATIVE LEADERSHIP

There's no denying that in some schools, one person exercises unilateral control over the anti-bullying work and that one person, perhaps a head teacher or perhaps the anti-bullying lead, is a bully himself … or herself. Just as with alpha females, some school leaders set their own agendas, constructed around self-centred ambition or perhaps a desire to exercise command and control. Worse still, some of these leaders gather a circle of like-minded bully leaders around them. It may sound unlikely, but I've seen this happen in some schools. And in these circumstances it's not only pupils and parents who begin to struggle with understanding what is and isn't acceptable behaviour in school; it's the staff as well.

A bullying leader can create a bewildering variety of unhealthy power dynamics between individual members and entire sections of the school community – for example, between individual teachers, between staff and management, between staff and pupils and between pupils. The negative impact is enormous, and if it's not challenged by a strong, collaborative approach, all trust will be eroded and inflexible authoritarianism and entrenched bullying will become the accepted norm. As a result, many members of staff will experience living in a culture of bullying in the same way that many students do.

There are shades of bullying and negative leadership that are not as destructive as those mentioned in the previous paragraph, yet which are nevertheless just as corrosive of trust and collaboration – for example, the negative impact that staff can have when they undermine or criticise other staff members in front of their pupils. Young people are acutely aware of how staff act towards each other and towards themselves. I've worked with children seriously affected by school staff deliberately seeking to draw them in to take sides against other staff members. Some of these pupils have described the experience as like being caught between two parents in a divorce struggle. The impact can be extremely uncomfortable, leaving them feeling torn and confused. Staff failing to lead by example, or failing to provide healthy models of pro-social behaviour, are other common elements of leadership gone awry in schools. All of these can be detrimental to pupils' behaviour and serve to encourage or reinforce antisocial norms.

If any member of the school community, whether as an individual or as part of a group, feels that they have been manipulated, marginalised, silenced or disempowered by insensitive or self-serving leadership, it's likely that there will be problems with anti-bullying work in that school. Actions that can be taken to reduce the risk of this happening, in addition to the journey towards collaboration and participation, include:

- Regular anti-bullying training for all staff.

- A consistent approach to reporting and acting on all incidents of bullying, agreed by all members of the school community.

- Checklists for pupils and staff about agreed and expected pro-social behaviours which are practised at all times in school.

- Encouraging and empowering every member of the school community to participate in all aspects of the development and application of anti-bullying work.

Of course, these measures are not guaranteed to change an authoritarian or bullying culture, especially where it's deeply embedded, but I have seen how over time their application in many schools where I've worked has brought about a shift in attitude.

TAKING THE LEAD: BUILDING A REPUTATION

A school's attitude towards bullying will be reflected in its reputation. The experiences of pupils and parents, and the stories they tell about that school, will form the basis of that reputation, alongside inspection reports. Without strong anti-bullying leadership, and a genuinely embedded anti-bullying ethos shared throughout the whole school community, there is a high risk that the school will develop a poor reputation. No one wants to send their child to a school that is reported to have a bullying culture. I have known many parents refuse to send their children to such a school.

A poor reputation not only impacts children and their parents; staff too will leave schools that have failed to implement effective anti-bullying strategies. And, of course, if the press get wind of problems like these, they can have a field day with lurid headlines and damning copy, further damaging the school's reputation. And those who suffer the most are the pupils, who have to survive in an environment that's failing to do everything within its power to safeguard them, educate them and develop them to their fullest potential.

The responsibility for embedding the good practice that a school's reputation is built on rests squarely with the SLT first and foremost, and then with all school staff. As I have argued, in order to put anti-bullying issues at the top of a school improvement agenda, open and honest discussions have to take place in a collaborative and participative atmosphere. Policies need to be in place, consistency established and energetic support clearly seen to be given to the anti-bullying leads.

It can also be very useful to involve members of the local community in the development of excellent strategies. For example, parents and other adults may have expertise in coaching, mentoring, counselling, negotiating and other such useful skills, and may be more than willing to come into school for an hour or so each week to share their expertise. Teachers don't need to think it's their job to do everything on their own, and pupils often appreciate external presenters delivering workshops. Schools are, after all, part of a wider social community. Another useful source of hands-on expertise can come from ex-pupils who have experienced the positive and negative aspects of the school at first hand. Why not actively involve them in the consultation process too? In addition, inviting community members into school as part of the consultation process can help to achieve a more balanced approach to the anti-bullying work, ensure that more voices are heard and challenge any entrenched behaviours or attempts to influence peer pressure or conformity.

The more people at school and in the community who are fully involved in creating or maintaining a school's positive reputation through excellent anti-bullying work, the better. Below is an exercise originally developed for staff anti-bullying training, but it can easily be adapted for others in the wider community to begin and then develop a discussion about reputation. Follow the discussion stage by listing actions for implementation.

- If you were a parent considering sending your child to this school, but were concerned about bullying, what questions what would you ask the school? And to whom would you address them?

- As a parent, would you have faith in the leadership of the school's response to bullying? Why, or why not?

- If you were a parent, what would you think of the school's anti-bullying web page? How could it be improved?

- If you were a child about to start school, and you asked a girl in Year 9 if there were any bullying problems there, what do you think you might be told?

- Imagine you were an interviewee for a staff position at the school and you spent a day as a fly on the staffroom wall before your interview, listening to the conversations and observing the behaviour of the teachers. What would your view of the school and the school leadership team be with regard to bullying behaviours?

- If you feel uncomfortable asking or answering any of these questions in a staff training session, ask yourself, *why?*

POSITIVE LEADERSHIP

The senior leadership team needs to be prepared to step back and take a strategic look at the whole school and what is most needed. While the SLT must take overall responsibility for the development, implementation and energetic support of the anti-bullying agenda, every member of the community also has a responsibility to lead by example. I call this *positive leadership* – the willingness to take personal (and sometimes collective) responsibility for whatever happens to us in our lives. Positive leadership is healthy for everyone involved. It's about considering the good of ourselves and of the whole community; it's about empowering staff, pupils and parents to feel part of the anti-bullying work; it's about empowering everyone to feel part of the anti-bullying ethos; it's about demonstrating positive role model behaviours; and it's about being willing to work as part of a whole school team to ensure a consistent approach to anti-bullying work.

SUMMARY

The SLT in schools is the foundation for building and developing a healthy approach that supports the culture, identity, reputation and ethos of the school. This is essential for the success of any anti-bullying policy. While the SLT is key to the establishment and development of this work, healthy leadership needs to be shared and supported by the whole school community. This will allow everyone to feel they are part of it, can own and contribute to it, and that it is a fair, just and transparent system of which they can be truly proud. In fact, ownership and pride in the leadership style should be an integral part of the whole school community approach. Ideally, this is what collaborative leadership and anti-bullying work should be all about. What this means in practice is that anyone across the whole school community should be able take a leadership role in anti-bullying work if they choose.

When the input is pro-social it will embed the anti-bullying ethos; however, if not everyone at school is supportive, it is very easy for the work to be undermined. To counter this threat, adults need to be positive role models for young people; that means parents, all school staff and the SLT. In girl bullying so many elements of anti-social behaviour are copied from negative role models, and so many incidents are left unreported, unsupported and unresolved, because those who should know better and act with greater responsibility are the ones who set the bad examples. Everybody needs to take responsibility, but it is the job of leadership in the first place to set an example and provide a cohesive and collaborative approach that tackles antisocial behaviour, and bullying in particular, with rigour and transparency.

In loco parentis is not just a duty, but a very useful metaphor to remind those who are charged with the education and safeguarding of young people that they should consider the needs of those in their care *as if they were their own children*. One of the key roles of a parent is to show fairness and consistency towards all their children, to set out clearly what boundaries are in place, what sanctions will be applied if those boundaries are transgressed and to make sure those sanctions are judiciously and fairly applied. Clear direction like this from the SLT plays a huge part in changing the ethos of the school and particularly in reducing incidents of bullying.

A consistent and collaborative approach allows everyone to know exactly where the goalposts are, where the lines are drawn and what happens if they're crossed. This is a healthy way to move anti-bullying work forward. When there is consistency in approach, modelled by an energetic and committed SLT, with clearly developed strategies shared by all and a school ethos that everyone can feel proud of, everyone will know exactly where they are and what they have to do. This can markedly reduce any frustration staff, pupils and parents might otherwise feel when they sense they are being unsupported or kept in the dark. In my view, anti-bullying work is not a role that one person takes on in isolation or that the SLT takes solely upon itself; it's the responsibility of the whole school community.

SUMMARY OF RESULTS OF THE 'DO I LOOK BOTHERED?' (DILB) SURVEY

RESPONSES

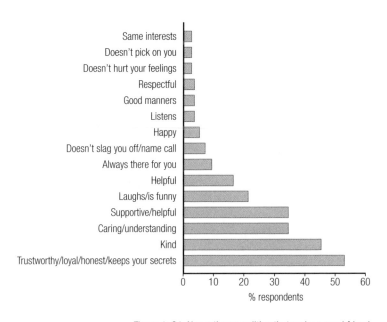

Figure 1: Q1. Name three qualities that make a good friend.

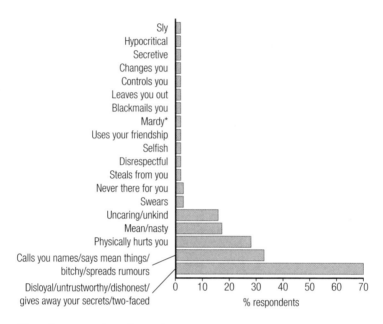

*For southerners: mardy = sulky, moody

Figure 2: Q2. Name three qualities that make a bad friend.

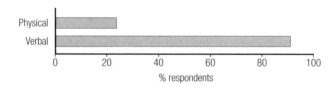

Figure 3: Q4. How do girls bully? What kind of things do they do?

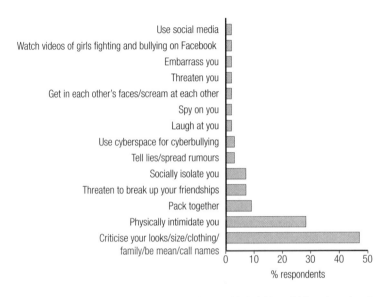

Figure 4: Q5. If you have seen girls bully, what kind of things did they do and say?

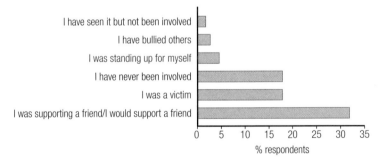

Figure 5: Q6. If you have ever been involved in girl bullying, can you think why you got involved?

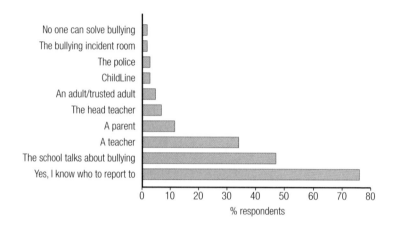

Figure 6: Q7. Does your school talk about bullying?
If so, do you know who or where you can report any bullying you have seen?

SPRINGBOARD QUESTIONS

This is a list of example springboard questions for use with whole school committees, open surveys or focus groups (from Chapter 8).

- How can we ensure that the anti-bullying committee is truly representative of the whole school community?

- How straightforwardly can we explain our views on the school's definition of bullying? (Use the school's current anti-bullying policy's definition as a trigger for discussion.)

- Which anti-bullying strategies work well, and which don't work so well?

- How can we increase the confidence of the whole school community in our commitment to addressing bullying behaviour?

- How can we support the perpetrator to make desirable changes in their bullying behaviour?

- What can we do to support victims of bullying?

- Who else do we need to support?

- How can we increase the faith that families have in the school's approach?

- How can members of the whole school community be consistently involved in anti-bullying work?

- How can the school establish and maintain an embedded anti-bullying ethos?

SUGGESTED QUESTIONS FOR DEVELOPING FOLLOW-UP SURVEYS OR FOCUS GROUPS

Follow-up surveys are best done once the committee has established a foundation for anti-bullying work using the findings and results from Appendix 1 (see Chapter 8).

- What is a clear definition that captures all types and methods of bullying?

- Discuss proactive strategies for early intervention and prevention that could be used in both direct and indirect bullying, including cyberbullying.

- Discuss reactive strategies or sanctions that could be used in both direct and indirect bullying, including cyberbullying, and that could be applied not just to perpetrators but also to victims, bystanders, reinforcers and supporters ('the pack').

- What are your ideas for long-term support for perpetrators, victims, bystanders, reinforcers and supporters ('the pack')?

- How can we help to support the anti-bullying ethos and ensure that everyone is doing their best to embed it consistently and constantly across the school community throughout the school year?

- How can everyone engage in addressing incidents of bullying at school, whether committed by students, staff or anyone else?

- Make a list of everything you think should be included in the anti-bullying policy.

- How can you make the school's anti-bullying policy as familiar, available and useful to every member of the school community as possible?

HINTS FOR DESIGNING AND RUNNING EFFECTIVE FOCUS GROUPS

A focus group (see Chapter 8) is a discussion facilitated by a focus group leader. It isn't an interview and shouldn't use structured interview questions. It should allow free-flowing discussion from the participants, so don't be tempted to write out a list of questions; that will only close down the process. All that is needed are keywords that will form the starting points for the discussion. The following steps are useful to bear in mind when preparing.

- Consider what will be the main points for discussion as *you* see them.

- Add any less obvious points that you may have left out, either because they didn't seem important or because they seemed too sensitive.

- Ask someone who will not be involved in the focus group which items *they* feel should be added to the list. It is better if this person is not involved in school management.

- If you have existing data collated from the school community (e.g. parent/pupil surveys) look at the issues raised and add any keywords that capture those issues.

- Include any issues raised in previous anti-bullying staff training sessions and pupil/parent consultation events.

Points to consider for design and structure:

- It takes more than one focus group to gather views that are representative of the whole school community.

- An effective focus group ideally consists of about eight people. More than eight and you run the risk that some people might not get a say or feel too intimidated to speak. My preference is to design for groups of between six and eight in order to reduce these problems and to allow sufficient time for everyone to make a meaningful contribution during a 30–45 minute slot. Of course, discretion for timing can be left in the hands of the group, depending on factors such as how much they have to contribute and how much time is available.

- Consider who will be in each focus group to ensure they complement each other. Think carefully about which students might intimidate certain other students and avoid such pairings.

- Be aware that dominant characters may try to hijack the session. Manage interactions in a way that allows everyone to contribute. For example, deliberately look towards the quieter participants and ease them into the conversations.

- Audio record the focus group so that the facilitator does not get distracted by having to write as well as listen. Recording means a number of key steps need to be taken, such as producing a consent form for participants to state their agreement to be recorded. The form should make it clear that:

> The recording will only be used to make notes.

> Anonymity will be guaranteed.

> The recording will be destroyed immediately the facilitator has used it for note-taking.

However:

> Confidentiality cannot be guaranteed as the views expressed will be used in the report of the session.

> With regard to confidentiality, *any safeguarding issues that arise must be passed on* to the appropriate authorities, by law.

Make sure everyone understands and agrees to the points and the implications before they sign.

On the day:

- *Before you begin to audio record*, introduce yourself and the aim of the focus group. Allow the group to introduce themselves.

- Introduce the main focus of the discussion and suggest some topics from the keyword list. However, be sure to allow the group to speak and let the discussion flow where it will. Keep an ear open for topics that begin to emerge.

- If certain salient topics aren't raised by the group, return to the keyword list if you think they are important.

- In my view, the facilitator should only be supportive and act as an interested party. Ideally, the participant's voices should account for *at least* 75% of the session. Avoid the temptation to intervene and interpret. Ask questions to clarify and deepen the discussion on emerging themes. It's the participants' views that should be gathered, not the facilitator's.

- Close the session by summing up the main points and asking if anyone has any more they would like to add. Clarify what the information will be used for and how it will be used. Ask if any participant would be happy to take part in further focus groups. Thank everyone for their time.

REFERENCES

Bishop, S. (2003a) Young people developing a repertoire of counselling psychology: talking theory. *Counselling Psychology*, 16, 95–103.

Bishop, S. (2003b) The development of peer support in secondary schools. *Pastoral Care*, June, 27–34.

Bishop, S. (2003c) *A Discursive Analysis of Training for Peer Support in Secondary Schools*. Published PhD. Nottingham Trent University.

Boronenko, V., Ucanok, Z., Slee, P., Campbell, M., Cross, D., Valimaki, M. and Spears, B. (2013) Training researchers: visits and training schools. In P. Smith and G. Steffgen (eds) *Cyberbullying Through the New Media*. Hove: Psychology Press, pp. 244–262.

Burgess-Proctor, A., Patchin, J.W. and Hinduja, S. (2010) Cyberbullying and online harassment: reconceptualising the victimisation of adolescent girls. In V. Garcia and J. Clifford (eds) *Female Crime Victims: Reality Reconsidered*. Upper Saddle River, NJ: Pearson, pp. 162–176.

Byron, T. (2008) *Safer Children in a Digital World: The Report of the Byron Review*. Nottingham: Department for Children, Schools and Families. Available at: http://webarchive.nationalarchives.gov.uk/20130401151715/ http://www.education.gov.uk/publications/eOrderingDownload/DCSF-00334-2008.pdf

Cartwright, N. (2007) *Peer Support Works: A Step-By-Step Guide to Long-Term Success*. London: Network Continuum Education.

ChildLine (2014) Experiences of 11–16-year-olds on social networking sites: a survey of young people's online experiences and coping strategies. Available at: www.nspcc.org.uk/services-and-resources/research-and-resources/experiences-of-11-16-year-olds-on-social-networking-sites/

Cross, E., Richardson, B., Douglas, T. and Vonkaenel-Flatt, J. (2009) *Virtual Violence: Protecting Children from Cyberbullying*. London: BeatBullying.

Department for Education (DfE) (2014a) *Preventing and Tackling Bullying: Advice for Headteachers, Staff and Governing Bodies*. London: DfE. Available at: https://www.gov.uk/government/uploads/system/uploads/attachment_data/file/444862/Preventing_and_tackling_bullying_advice.pdf

Department for Education (DfE) (2014b) School support for children and young people who are bullied [fact sheet]. Available at: https://www.gov.uk/government/uploads/system/uploads/attachment_data/file/444864/Supporting_bullied_children.pdf

Department for Education (DfE) (2015) *Keeping Children Safe in Education: Statutory Guidence for Schools and Colleges*. London: DfE. Available at: https://www.gov.uk/government/uploads/system/uploads/attachment_data/file/435939/Keeping_children_safe_in_education.pdf

Dickerson, M.S. (2011) Building a collaborative school culture using appreciative inquiry. *Journal of Arts, Science & Commerce*, 2(2), 25–36.

Ditch the Label (2014) Annual bullying survey. Available at: www.ditchthelabel.org/annual-bullying-survey-2014/

Duncan, N. and Owens, L. (2011) Bullying, social power and heteronormativity: girls constructions of popularity. *Children and Society*, 25, 306–316.

Girl Scout Research Institute (2011) Real to me: girls and reality TV [fact sheet]. Available at: www.girlscouts.org/content/dam/girlscouts-gsusa/forms-and-documents/about-girl-scouts/research/real_to_me_factsheet.pdf

Hinduja, S. and Patchin, J.W. (2008) Cyberbullying: an exploratory analysis of factors related to offending and victimisation. *Deviant Behaviour*, 29(2), 1–29.

Jiang, D., Walsh, M. and Leena, K.A. (2011) The linkage between child-hood bullying behaviour and future offending. *Criminal Behaviour and Mental Health*, 21, 128–135.

Ofsted (2014) *Inspecting Safeguarding in Maintained Schools and Academies.* Ref: 140143. Available at: www.gov.uk/government/uploads/system/uploads/attachment_data/file/457203/Inspecting_safeguarding_in_maintained_schools_and_academies_-_a_briefing_for_section_5_inspections.pdf

Olweus, D. (1978) *Aggression in Schools: Bullies and Whipping Boys.* Washington, DC: Hemisphere.

Olweus, D. (1993) *Bullying at School: What We Know and What We Can Do.* Oxford: Blackwell.

Saaty, T. (2008) Conflict resolution as a game with priorities: multidimensional cardinal payoffs – Part 1. *Risk Analysis Theory & Applications*, 1, 8–21.

Sherer, J.Z. (2008) Power in distributed leadership: how teacher agency influences instructional leadership practice. Paper presented at the American Educational Research Association annual meeting: Research on Schools, Neighborhoods, and Communities: Toward Civic Responsibility, New York, 24–28 March.

Smith, P.K. (2014) *Understanding School Bullying: Its Nature and Prevention Strategies.* London: Sage Publications.

Smith, P.K., Steffgen, G. and Sittichai, R. (2013) The nature of cyberbullying, and an international network in P. K. Smith and G. Steffgen (eds) *Cyberbullying Through the New Media: Findings from an International Network.* Hove: Psychology Press pp. 3–20.

Zimbardo, P.G. (2007) *The Lucifer Effect: How Good People Turn Evil.* New York: Random House.

BIBLIOGRAPHY

Barker, J. and Hodes, D. (2004) *The Child in Mind: A Child Protection Handbook.* Oxford: Routledge.

Bee, H. (1994) *Lifespan Development.* New York: HarperCollins.

Byron, T. (2009) Impact on victims. In E. Cross, B. Richardson, T. Douglas and J. Vonkaenel-Flatt (eds) *Virtual Violence: Protecting Children from Cyberbullying.* London: BeatBullying.

Coloroso, B. (2003) *The Bully, the Bullied and the Bystander: From Pre-School to Secondary School – How Parents and Teachers Can Help Break the Cycle of Violence.* New York: HarperCollins.

Cowie, H. and Jennifer, D. (2008) *New Perspectives on Bullying.* Maidenhead: McGraw-Hill.

Department of Health (1999) *Children's Needs – Parenting Capacity: The Impact of Parental Mental Illness, Problem Alcohol and Drug Use, and Domestic Violence on Children's Development.* London: HMSO.

Duncan, N. (2014) Schooling, bullying and disability: how schools can make things worse. Presented at *Journal of Research in Special Educational Needs* invitation research seminar, Nottingham, October 2014. Conference paper.

Ginnis, P. (2004) *The Teacher's Toolkit: Raise Classroom Achievement with Strategies for Every Learner.* Carmarthen: Crown House Publishing.

Glover, D., Cartwright, N. and Gleeson, D. (1998) *Towards Bully-Free Schools: Interventions in Action.* Buckingham: Open University Press.

Horwath, J. (ed.) (2001) *The Child's World: Assessing Children in Need.* London: Jessica Kingsley Publishers.

Hughes, L. and Owen, H. (2009) *Good Practice in Safeguarding Children: Working Effectively in Child Protection.* London: Jessica Kingsley Publishing.

Jones, S.E., Bombieri, L., Livingstone, A.G. and Manstead, S.R. (2012) The influences of norms and social identities on children's responses to bullying. *British Journal of Educational Psychology*, 82, 241–256.

Kohut, M.R. (2007) *The Complete Guide to Understanding, Controlling, and Stopping Bullies and Bullying: A Complete Guide for Teachers and Parents.* Ocala, FL: Atlantic Publishing Group.

Perry, A. (ed.) (2009) *Teenagers and Attachment: Helping Adolescents Engage with Life and Learning.* London: Worth Publishing.

Raymond, A. (2009) *The Child Protection and Safeguarding Handbook for Schools: A Comprehensive Guide to Policy and Practice.* Salisbury: Baskerville Press.

Richardson, R. and Miles, B. (2008) *Racist Incidents and Bullying in Schools: How to Prevent Them and How to Respond When They Happen.* Stoke-on-Trent: Trentham Books.

INDEX

OSIRIS
EDUCATIONAL

Osiris Educational is the UK's leading independent provider of professional development for teachers.

Osiris believes that every child should receive a world class education. Helping teachers in their continuous development is the crucial step to achieving this. We work at the forefront of innovation in education providing pioneering, challenging and effective training solutions.

More than 400 presenters work with Osiris Educational to help teachers improve their ways of thinking and their approaches to teaching.

Some of the most renowned trainers from across the world work with Osiris Educational including: Professor John Hattie, Professor Barry Hymer, Dr Bill Rogers, Dr Angela Duckworth, Professor Carol Dweck, Andy Griffith and Mark Burns.

Our 5 crucial paths to CPD training cover everything from Early Years through to Key Stage Five.

Day Courses:
- Leadership and Management
- Teaching and Learning
- Pastoral and Behavioural
- SEN and Gifted and Talented
- Curriculum
- Ofsted

In-School Training:
- Early Years
- Primary
- Secondary

Teacher and Leadership Programmes:
- Outstanding Teaching Intervention
- Visible Learning
- Mindsets

Conferences and Keynotes:
- Leading Speakers
- Key Issues and Policies

Fast Updates:
- Twilights
- Policy Briefings

**FOR MORE INFORMATION CALL 0808 160 5 160
OR VISIT OSIRISEDUCATIONAL.CO.UK**